WHEN AFRICA AWAKES

WHEN AFRICA AWAKES

FIRST PUBLISHED IN 1920

HUBERT HENRY HARRISON

WITH AN INTRODUCTION BY JOHN HENRIK CLARKE

Black Classic Press
Baltimore

When Africa Awakes
First Published 1920
Published by Black Classic Press 1997
Introduction Copyright 1997 by John Henrik Clarke
All Rights Reserved. Published 1997

Library of Congress Card Catalog Number: 96-83451
ISBN 0-933121-56-3 (paper)
ISBN 0-993121-88-1 (cloth)
Cover design by Laurie Williams/A Street Called Straight

Founded in 1978, Black Classic Press specializes in bringing to light
obscure and significant works by and about people of African descent.
If our books are not available in your area, ask your local bookseller to
order them. Our current list of titles can be obtained by writing:

Black Classic Press
c/o List
P.O. Box 13414
Baltimore, MD 21203

A Young Press With Some Very Old Ideas

Visit us on the world wide web at www.blackclassic.com

Distributed by Publishers Group West

**This book was reprinted from the best
copy of the original available.**

INTRODUCTION

Harrison was not only perhaps the foremost Afro-American intellect of his time, but one of America's greatest minds. No one worked more seriously and indefatigably to enlighten his fellowmen: none of the Afro-American leaders of his time had a saner and more effective program—but others, unquestionably his inferiors, received the recognition that was his due. Even today but a very small proportion of the Negro intelligentsia has ever heard of him.

—*World's Great Men of Color,* vol. 2
(New York: J.A. Rogers, 1947), 611.

New interest in the life and work of Hubert Harrison is appropriate. In his lifetime, he was an advanced thinker and a prophet. Carefully read today, *When Africa Awakes* shows that Hubert Harrison is even ahead of our time. Had the generation of African Americans who knew him listened to what he was saying, many of the tragic dilemmas in the African world probably would not exist. He was a man for the seasons of his lifetime and for all seasons. Reading *When Africa Awakes* today is somewhat alarming when one considers that this book was written in 1920. Politically, Africa did awaken in 1957 when the former Gold Coast colony of West Africa reemerged as Ghana. The African independence explosion was underway. Africa had awakened with a great dream of unity, prosperity, and a new destiny for itself and for all mankind. Within the next two decades, miseducated Africans and colonial and neocolonial saboteurs would turn Africa's dream into the tragic nightmare we behold today.

As a people, we have not carefully listened to our greatest messengers. Harrison was one of them. We should read *When Africa Awakes* for an understanding of what Harrison was saying to the African world of his day and what he still has to say to the contemporary African world. Hubert Harrison (1883—1927) lived and was active during the formative period of Marcus Garvey's Universal Negro Improvement Association. He had the privilege of introducing Marcus Garvey to his first large audience in Harlem. Harlem and African people everywhere were Harrison's window on the world. His general knowledge was as expansive as his specific knowledge about his own people and the role they have played in the world and should play in the future. He was a socialist until he discovered that most socialists are not true to the teachings of socialism. Harrison was a highly spiritual person who was suspicious of all forms of organized religion. A self-trained man who was better trained than any college of his day would have trained him, Harrison demonstrated that he recognized education as a potent weapon in the battle for liberation. He called for the kind of practical education that the schools of his day would not consider because it was education for the responsible handling of power.

Hubert Harrison was also a founder of the Liberty League, a standard bearer of what a Black pressure lobby should be. Like all good agitators, he called attention to neglected issues and causes. He did not resolve all the problems that he put on his agenda, but he developed a propaganda approach that made a large number of people consider problems and situations that they would have otherwise ignored. He understood that the role of the political educator is to call attention to the smoldering fires that threaten the times, even if he cannot put the fires out.

In "Democracy and Race Friction," Harrison calls attention to the contradictions within the concept of democracy in the United States as it relates to different racial groups in America. In his writings and speeches, he dared to remove the political mask and to expose the fact that the country was actually founded as a haven for middle and upper class white protestant property-owning males who were committed to the status quo. Politically and economically, the rest of America fell in line behind that group. That original design of American democracy has changed very little, if at all, since the Founding Fathers brought it into being.

In the chapter "The Negro and the War," Hubert Harrison, like W. E. B. Du Bois, examines World War I and calls attention to the African roots of that war both at home and abroad. After the war, Black American soldiers were told that their lot would not be changed appreciably although they had fought in the war. The Ku Klux Klan was rampant in the land, and job discrimination and job denial made no exception of Black veterans coming home from the war. There were riots all over the United States. Because of the many riots and the blood spilled, the summer of 1919 was called Red Summer. This created the atmosphere in which Marcus Garvey's dream of African redemption and African return could and did flourish. The Garvey movement, preaching hope and directing the attention of Black Americans toward Africa, began to emerge. As a writer for Garvey's newspaper the *Negro World,* and later one of its editors, Hubert Harrison was an important theoretical interpreter of American history during this critical period.

In his essay "The New Politics," Harrison called for an independent Black political thrust, a role for Black people different from that envisioned by Republicans and Democrats. Harrison knew that Blacks were not getting anything but worn out political hand-me-downs from both parties—tokens that could be converted into nothing except more frustration. He called for the kind of education that would prepare African people for nationhood. Harrison's voice was strong, and his message was clear. He realized that on the road to freedom leading to the restoration of manhood, womanhood, and national destiny there were no stop signs and few resting places. He was a rebel who understood that in a situation of crisis revolution for change is a full-time commitment. Hubert Harrison dealt with the recurring issue of African American leadership at a time when the second generation after Emancipation was becoming self-seeking individuals rather than people-leaders. He dared to speak out and ask: "Leaders, where are you leading us and for whom?"; "Leaders, whom are you committed to, and who is your paymaster?"

Harrison's article "The New Race Consciousness" that includes "An Open Letter to the Socialist Party" is still relevant, but it should also address the Communist Party. Too many people have developed strategies for our agenda without first consulting us. Hubert Harrison knew that a revolutionary socialist party could not emerge in America if Black Americans were on the sidelines watching the political parade. If any party was to be effective among us, he argued, Blacks would have to be a part of the decision-making apparatus of that party. Jesse Jackson may have learned this lesson, but I for one have my doubts.

To this day, we have not solved the issue Hubert Harrison discusses in his article "Race First." We are divided in our loyalty. Some Blacks wearing the badge of nationalism are really opportunists in the pay of our enemy. The left movement, both socialist and communist, thought that class prevailed over race. In the never-never-land of their political dreams, maybe it does; but in the West, the reality is that race rules over class. In 1903, W. E. B. Du Bois reminded us that the problem of the twentieth century was the color line. By extension, I would add that we are also faced with the problem of the political line and the cultural line.

In my opinion, the essence of what Hubert Harrison was saying and is still saying to us is that there can be no freedom without responsibility—that all proper education is an education for liberation and that when Africa awakens, Africa's own sons and daughters must be the masters and the managers of every aspect of their nation, including its vast mineral wealth. No people can be truly sovereign if the wealth generating resources of the country are managed by former colonial masters. With the reissuing *When Africa Awakes,* the strong and clear voice of Hubert Harrison is speaking to us again. I hope this time we will listen. Let us try to complete the important theoretical work that he started.

—John Henrik Clarke

HUBERT H. HARRISON

TABLE OF CONTENTS

INTRODUCTORY

The Great War of 1914-1918 has served to liberate many new ideas undreamt of by those who rushed humanity into that bath of blood. During that war the idea of democracy was widely advertised, especially in the English-speaking world; mainly as a convenient camouflage behind which competing imperialists 'masked their sordid aims. Even the dullest can now see that those who so loudly proclaimed and formulated the new democratic demands never had the slightest intention of extending either the limits or the applications of "democracy." Ireland and India, Egypt and Russia are still the Ithuriel's spear of the great democratic pretence. The flamboyant advertising of "democracy" has returned to plague the inventors; for the subject populations who contributed their millions in men and billions in treasure for the realization of the ideal which was flaunted before their eyes are now clamoring for their share of it. They are demanding that those who advertised democracy shall now make good. This is the main root of that great unrest which is now troubling the decrepit statesmanship of Europe and America. But the rigid lines of the old

regime will not permit the granting of these new demands. Hence the new war against democracy which expresses itself in the clever but futile attempt to outlaw the demands for fuller freedom as "sedition" and "Bolshevism."

The most serious aspect of this new situation is the racial one. The white world has been playing with the catch-words of democracy while ruthlessly ruling an overwhelming majority of black, brown and yellow peoples to whom these catchwords were never intended to apply. But these many-colored millions have taken part in the war "to make the world safe for democracy," and they are now insisting that democracy shall be made safe for them. This, in plain English, their white overlords do not intend to concede. "The undictated development of all peoples" was, at best, intended "for white people only." Thus, white civilization is brought face to face with a crisis out of which may easily grow military conflicts of tremendous scope and, more remotely, the passing of international control out of the hands of a few white nations.

The tenseness of this new situation has been reflected here in the United States in the mental attitude of the Negro people. They have developed new ideas of their own place in the category of races and have evolved new conceptions of their powers and destiny. These ideas have quickened their race-consciousness and they are making new demands on themselves, on their leaders and on the white people in whose midst they live. These new demands apply to politics, domestic and international, to education and culture, to commerce and industry.

It seems proper that the white people of America should know what these demands are and should understand the spirit in which they are being urged. Obviously, it is not well that they should be misrepresented and lied about. Futile fulminations about the spread of "Bolshevism" among Negroes by "agitators" will not help toward an understanding of this new phenomenon. They can but befog the issues and defer the dawning of a better day. On the other hand, the Negro people will profit by a clarified presentation of their own side of the case. It is to meet this dual need that this little book is launched.

It is a compilation of some of the author's contributions to Negro journalism between 1917 and the present year and consists of selected editorials, special articles and reviews written for *The Voice, The New Negro,* and *The Negro World.* I have selected for reproduction those only which could fairly be considered as expositions of the new point of view evolved during the Great War and coming into prominence since the peace was signed. So far, this point of view has not been fully presented—by the Negro. White men, like Messrs. Sandburg and Seligman, have essayed to interpret it to the white world. This little volume presents directly that which they would interpret.

It may seem unusual to put into permanent form the deliverances of this species of literature. But I venture to think that, as literature, they will stand the test; and I am willing to assume the risks. Besides, I feel that I owe it to my people to preserve this cross-section of their new-found soul. It was my privilege to assist in shaping some of the forms of the new consciousness; and to preserve for posterity a portion of its record has seemed a duty which should not be shirked.

It was in 1916 that I first began to hammer out some of the ideas which will be found in these pages. It was in that year that I gave up my work as a lecturer and teacher among white people to give myself exclusively to work among my own people. In the summer of 1917, with the financial aid of many poor but willing hearts I brought out *The Voice,* the first Negro journal of the new dispensation, and, for some time, the only one. *The Voice* failed in March, 1919; but in the meanwhile it had managed to make an indelible impression. Many of the writings reproduced here are taken from its files. The others are from *The Negro World,* of which I assumed the joint editorship in January of this year. A few appeared in *The New Negro,* a monthly magazine which I edited for a short time.

The account of the launching of the Liberty League is given here in the first chapter because *that meeting at historic Bethel on June* 12, 1917, *and the labors of tongue and pen out of which that meeting emerged were the foundation for the mighty structures of racial propaganda which have been raised since then.* This is a fact not generally known because I have not hankered after newspaper publicity.

It is hardly necessary to point out that the AFRICA of the title is to be taken in its racial rather than in its geographical sense.   HUBERT H. HARRISON.

New York, August 15, 1920.

WHEN AFRICA AWAKES

CHAPTER I.

THE BEGINNINGS.

Launching the Liberty League

(*From The Voice of July* 4, 1917.)

The Liberty League of Negro-Americans, which was recently organized by the Negroes of New York, presents the most startling program of any organization of Negroes in the country today. This is nothing less than the demand that the Negroes of the United States be given a chance to enthuse over democracy for themselves in America before they are expected to enthuse over democracy in Europe. The League is composed of "Negro-Americans, loyal to their country in every respect, and obedient to her laws."

The League has an interesting history. It grew out of the labors of Mr. Hubert H. Harrison, who has been on the lecture platform for years and is well and favorably known to thousands of white New Yorkers from Wall Street to Washington Heights.

Two years ago Mr. Harrison withdrew from an international political organization, and, a little more than a year ago, gave up lecturing to white people, to devote himself to lecturing exclusively among his own people. He acquired so much influence among them that when he issued the first call for a mass-meeting "to protest against lynching in the land of liberty and disfranchisement in the home of democracy," although the call was not advertised in any newspaper, the church in which the meeting was held was packed from top to bottom. At this mass-meeting, which was held at Bethel Church on June 12, the organization was effected and funds were raised to sustain it and to extend its work all over the country.

Harrison was subsequently elected its president, with Edgar

Grey and James Harris as secretary and treasurer, respectively. At the close of this mass-meeting he hurriedly took the midnight train for Boston, where a call for a similar meeting had been issued by W. Monroe Trotter, editor of *The Boston Guardian*. While there he delivered an address in Fanueil Hall, the cradle of American liberty, and told the Negroes of Boston what their brothers in New York had done and were doing. The result was the linking up of the New York and the Boston organizations, and Harrison was elected chairman of a national committee of arrangements to issue a call to every Negro organization in the country to send delegates to a great race-congress which is to meet in Washington in September or October and put their grievances before the country and Congress.

At the New York mass-meeting money was subscribed for the establishment of a newspaper to be known as *The Voice* and to serve as the medium of expression for the new demands and aspirations of the new Negro. It was made clear that this "New Negro Movement" represented a breaking away of the Negro masses from the grip of the old-time leaders—none of whom was represented at the meeting. The audience rose to their feet with cheers when Harrison was introduced by the chairman. The most striking passages of his speech were those in which he demanded that Congress make lynching a Federal crime and take the Negro's life under national protection, and declared that since lynching was murder and a violation of Federal and State laws, it was incumbent upon the Negroes themselves to maintain the majesty of the law and put down the law-breakers by organizing all over the South to defend their own lives whenever their right to live was invaded by mobs which the local authorities were too weak or unwilling to suppress.

The meeting was also addressed by Mr. J. C. Thomas, Jr., a young Negro lawyer, who pointed out the weakness and subserviency of the old-time political leaders and insisted that Negroes stop begging for charity in the matter of their legal rights and demand justice instead.

Mr. Marcus Garvey, president of the Jamaica Improvement Association, was next introduced by Mr. Harrison. He spoke in enthusiastic approval of the new movement and pledged it his hearty support.

After the Rev. Dr. Cooper, the pastor of Bethel, had addressed the meeting, the following resolutions were adopted and a petition to Congress was prepared and circulated. In addition the meeting sent a telegram to the Jews of Russia, congratulating them upon the acquisition of full political and civil rights and expressing the hope that the United States might soon follow the democratic example of Russia.

Resolutions Passed at the Liberty League Meeting

Two thousand Negro-Americans assembled in mass-meeting at Bethel A. M. E. Church to protest against lynching in the land of liberty and disfranchisement in the home of democracy have, after due deliberation, adopted the following resolutions and make them known to the world at large in the earnest hope that whenever the world shall be made safe for democracy our corner of that world will not be forgotten.

We believe that this world war will and must result in a larger measure of democracy for the peoples engaged therein— whatever may be the secret ambitions of their several rulers.

We therefore ask, first, that when the war shall be ended and the council of peace shall meet to secure to every people the right to rule their own ancestral lands free from the domination of tyrants, domestic and foreign, the similar rights of the 250,000,000 Negroes of Africa be conceded. Not to concede them this is to lay the foundation for more wars in the future and to saddle the new democracies with the burden of a militarism greater than that under which the world now groans.

Secondly, we, as Negro-Americans who have poured out our blood freely in every war of the Republic, and upheld her flag with undivided loyalty, demand that since we have shared to the full measure of manhood in bearing the burdens of democracy we should also share in the rights and privileges of that democracy.

And we believe that the present time, when the hearts of ninety millions of our white fellow-citizens are aflame with the passionate ardor of democracy which has carried them into the greatest war of the age with the sole purpose of suppressing autocracy in Europe, is the best time to appeal to them to give to twelve millions of us the elementary rights of democracy at home.

For democracy, like charity, begins at home, and we find it hard to endure without murmur and with the acquiescence of our government the awful evils of lynching, which is a denial of the right to life; of segregation, Jim Crowism and peonage, which are a denial of the right to liberty; and disfranchisement, which is a denial of justice and democracy.

And since Imperial Russia, formerly the most tyrannous government in Europe, has been transformed into Republican Russia, whereby millions of political serfs have been lifted to the level of citizenship rights; since England is offering the meed of political manhood to the hitherto oppressed Irish and the down-trodden Hindu; and since these things have helped to make good the democratic assertions of these countries of the old world now engaged in war;

Therefore, be it resolved:

That we, the Negro people of the first republic of the New World, ask all true friends of democracy in this country to help us to win these same precious rights for ourselves and our children.

That we invite the government's attention to the great danger which threatens democracy through the continued violation of the 13th, 14th and 15th amendments, which is a denial of justice and the existence of mob-law for Negroes from Florida to New York;

That we intend to protest and to agitate by every legal means until we win these rights from the hands of our government and induce it to protect democracy from these dangers, and square the deeds of our nation with its declarations;

That we create adequate instruments for securing these ends and make our voice heard and heeded in the councils of our country, and

That copies of these resolutions be forwarded to the Congress of the United States and to such other public bodies as shall seem proper to us.

The Liberty League's Petition to the House of Representatives of the United States, July 4, 1917

We, the Negro people of the United States, loyal to our country in every respect, and obedient to her laws, respectfully petition your honorable body for a redress of the specific grievances and flagrant violations of your own laws as set forth in this statement.

We beg to call your attention to the discrepancy which exists between the public profession of the government that we are lavishing our resources of men and money in this war in order to make the world safe for democracy, and the just as public performances of lynching-bees, Jim-crowism and disfranchisement in which our common country abounds.

We should like to believe in our government's professions of democracy, but find it hard to do so in the presence of the facts; and we judge that millions of other people outside of the country will find it just as hard.

Desirous, therefore, of squaring our country's profession with her performance, that she may not appear morally contemptible in the eyes of friends and foes alike, we, the Negro people of the United States, who have never been guilty of any disloyalty or treason to our government, demand that the nation shall justify to the world her assertions of democracy by setting free the millions of Negroes in the South from political and civil slavery through the enactment of laws which will either take the Negroes under the direct protection of the U. S. Congress by making lynching a Federal crime, or (by legislative mandate) compelling the several States which now deprive the Negroes of their right to self-government, to give them the suffrage as Russia has done for her Jews. We ask this in the name of the American declaration that the world shall be made safe for democracy and fervently pray that your honorable body will not go back upon democracy.

CHAPTER II.

DEMOCRACY AND RACE FRICTION.

The East St. Louis Horror

This nation is now at war to make the world "safe for democracy," but the Negro's contention in the court of public opinion is that until this nation itself is made safe for twelve million of its subjects the Negro, at least, will refuse to believe in the democratic assertions of the country. The East St. Louis pogrom gives point to this contention. Here, on the eve of the celebration of the Nation's birthday of freedom and equality, the white people, who are denouncing the Germans as Huns and barbarians, break loose in an orgy of unprovoked and villainous barbarism which neither Germans nor any other civilized people have ever equalled.

How can America hold up its hands in hypocritical horror at foreign barbarism while the red blood of the Negro is clinging to those hands? so long as the President and Congress of the United States remain dumb in the presence of barbarities in their own land which would tip their tongues with righteous indignation if they had been done in Belgium, Ireland or Galicia?

And what are the Negroes to do? Are they expected to re-echo with enthusiasm the patriotic protestations of the boot-licking leaders whose pockets and positions testify to the power of the white man's gold? Let there be no mistake. Whatever the Negroes may be compelled by law to do and say, the resentment in their hearts will not down. Unbeknown to the white people of this land a temper is being developed among Negroes with which the American people will have to reckon.

At the present moment it takes this form: If white men are to kill unoffending Negroes, Negroes must kill white men in defense of their lives and property. This is the lesson of the East St. Louis massacre.

The press reports declare that, "the troops who were on duty during the most serious disturbances were ordered not to shoot." The civil and military authorities are evidently winking at the work of the mobs—horrible as that was—and the Negroes of the city need not look to them for protection. They must protect themselves. And even the United States Supreme Court concedes them this right.

There is, in addition, a method of retaliation which we urge upon them. It is one which will hit those white men who have the power to prevent lawlessness just where they will feel it most, in the place where they keep their consciences—the pocket-book. Let every Negro in East St. Louis and the other cities where race rioting occurs draw his money from the savings-bank and either bank it in the other cities or in the postal savings bank. The only part of the news reports with which we are well pleased is that which states that the property loss is already estimated at a million and a half of dollars.

Another reassuring feature is the one suppressed in most of the news dispatches. We refer to the evidences that the East St. Louis Negroes organized themselves during the riots and fought back under some kind of leadership. We Negroes will never know, perhaps, how many whites were killed by our enraged brothers in East St. Louis. It isn't the news-policy of the white newspapers (whether friendly or unfriendly) to spread such news broadcast. It might teach Negroes too much. But we will hope for the best.

The occurrence should serve to enlarge rapidly the membership of The Liberty League of Negro-Americans which was organized to take practical steps to help our people all over the land in the protection of their lives and liberties.—July 4th, 1917.

"Arms and the Man"

In its editorial on "The East St. Louis Horror" *The Voice* said:

How can America hold up its hands in hypocritical horror at foreign barbarism while the red blood of the Negro is clinging to those hands? So long as the President and Congress of the United States remain dumb in the presence of barbarities in their own land which would tip their tongues with righteous indignation if they had been done in Belgium, Ireland or Galicia?

And what are the Negroes to do? Are they expected to re-echo with enthusiasm the patriotic protestations of the boot-licking leaders whose pockets and positions testify to the power of the white man's gold? Let there be no mistake. Whatever the Negroes may be compelled by law to do and say, the resentment in their hearts will not down. *Unbeknown to the white people of this land a temper is being developed among Negroes with which the American people will have to reckon.*

At the present moment it takes this form: If white men are to kill unoffending Negroes, Negroes must kill white men in defence of their lives and property. This is the lesson of the East St. Louis massacre.

To this, the New York *Age* makes reply in two ways. Its editor, in an interview given to the *Tribune*, declares that:

The representative Negro does not approve of radical socialistic outbursts, such as calling upon the Negroes to defend themselves against the whites.

And in its editorial of last week it insists that:

No man, or woman either, for that matter, is a friend to the race, who publicly advises a resort to violence to redress the wrongs and injustices to which members of the race are subjected in various sections of the country at the present time.

The Negro race is afflicted with many individuals whose wagging tongues are apt to lead them into indiscreet utterances that reflect upon the whole race. . . . The unruly tongues should not be allowed to alienate public sympathy from the cause of the oppressed.

Now, although *The Voice* seeks no quarrel with *The Age,* we are forced to dissent from this cringing, obsequious view which it champions. And we do this on the ground that cringing has gone out of date, that *The Age's* view does not now represent any influential or important section of Negro opinion. The group which once held that view went to pieces when Dr. Washington died. The *white* papers in their news items of last week gave instance after instance showing that Negroes not only counselled self-defense, but actually practiced it. (And *The Age,* by the way, was the only *Negro* paper in New York City which excluded these items from its news columns.) If the press reports are correct, then *The Voice* told the simple truth when it spoke of the new temper which was being developed "unbeknown to the white people of this land." And an outsider might conclude that *The Voice* was a better friend to the white people by letting them know this, than *The Age* was by trying to lie about it.

But the controversy goes much deeper than the question of candor and truthfulness. *The Age* and *The Voice* join issue on this double question: Have Negroes a right to defend themselves against whites? Should they defend themselves? (And this, of course, means violence.) *The Voice* answers, "Yes!" *The Age* answers "No!" Who is to decide? Let us appeal to the courts. Every law-book and statute-book, every court in the civilized world and in the United States agree that every *human* being has the legal as well as moral right to kill those who attack and try to kill him.   Then the question for *The Age* to decide, is whether Negroes are human beings.   To call our view "socialistic" is to call the courts "socialistic," and displays an amazing ignorance both of Socialism and of human nature.

Before we leave this question, it is proper to consider the near and remote consequences of the radical view. *The Age* says that unruly tongues will alienate public sympathy from the oppressed.   Good God!   Isn't it high time to ask of what value is that kind of sympathy which is ready to be alienated as soon as Negroes cease to be "niggers" and insist on being men?   Is that the sort of sympathy on which *The Age* has thrived?   Then we will have none of it.

And, as to the remoter consequences: neither we nor *The Age* has a lease on the future.   We can but prophesy. But intelligent people reach the unknown via the known, and prophesy the future from the known past and present. And we do know that no race or group of people past or present ever won to the status of manhood among men by yielding up that right which even a singed cat will not yield up—the right to defend their lives.   If *The Age* knows of any instance to the contrary in the history of the past seven thousand years, let it mention that instance. But *The Age* may ask:

"What will self defense accomplish?"   Let us see first what the absence of self-defense accomplishes.   In its news account of the St. Louis massacre, the *Amsterdam News* shows that whenever the white mobs found a group of Negroes organized and armed, *they turned back;*

while *The Age* itself had this significant and pathetic sentence:

Since the massacre, which will go down in history alongside the atrocities committed in Brussels and Rheims, a delegation of Negroes has held a conference with Governor Lowden at Springfield, *but the outcome of this meeting will not bring back the lives of those who, for no valid reason, were struck down and murdered in cold blood.*

Taking the two things together the answer seems clear enough. When murder is cheap murder is indulged in recklessly; when it is likely to be costly it is not so readily indulged in. Will *The Age* venture to deny this? No? Then we say, let Negroes help to make murder costly, for by so doing they will aid the officers of the city, state and nation in instilling respect for law and order into the minds of the worst and lowest elements of our American cities. And we go further: We say that it is not alone the brutality of the whites—it is also the cowardice of Negroes and the lickspittle leadership of the last two decades which, like *The Age,* told us to "take it all lying down"—it is this which has been the main reason for our "bein' so aisily lynched," as Mr. Dooley puts it.

Whatever *The Age* may say, Negroes will fight back as they are already fighting back. And they will be more highly regarded—as are the Irish—because of fighting back.

We are aiming at the white man's respect—not at his sympathy. We cannot win that respect by any conspicuous and contemptible cowardice; the only kind of sympathy which we may win by that is the kind of sympathy which men feel for a well-kicked dog which cringes while they kick it.

"Rights are to be won by those who are ready and willing to fight, if necessary, to have those rights respected."

Who says this? Theodore Roosevelt. So does President
Wilson. So does the U. S. Government. That is why
we went to war with Germany. Our country always acts
upon the best and highest principle and we Negroes have
just begun to see that our country is quite right. Therefore, we are willing to follow its glorious example. That
is all.

————

The Negro and the Labor Unions

There are two kinds of labor unionism; the A. F. of L.
kind and the other kind. So far, the Negro has been
taught to think that all unionism was like the unionism
of the American Federation of Labor, and because of this
ignorance, his attitude toward organized labor has been
that of the scab. For this no member of the A. F. of L.
can blame the Negro. The policy of that organization
toward the Negro has been damnable. It has kept him
out of work and out of the unions as long as it could;
and when it could no longer do this it has taken him in,
tricked him, and discriminated against him.

On the other hand, the big capitalists who pay low
wages (from the son of Abraham Lincoln in the Pullman
Co. to Julius Rosenwald of the Sears Roebuck Co.)
have been rather friendly to the Negro. They have given
their money to help him build Y. M. C. A.'s and schools
of a certain type. They have given him community help
in Northern cities and have expended charity on him—
and on the newspapers and parsons who taught him.
Small wonder, then, that the Negro people are anti-union.

Labor unions were created by white working men that
they might bring the pressure of many to bear upon the
greedy employer and make him give higher wages and
better living conditions to the laborer. When they, in

turn, become so greedy that they keep out the majority of working people, by high dues and initiation fees, they no longer represent the interests of the laboring class. They stand in the way of this class's advancement—*and they must go.* They must leave the way clear for the 20th century type of unionism which says: "To leave a single worker out is to leave something for the boss to use against us. Therefore we must organize in One Big Union of *all* the working-class." This is the type of unionism which organized, in 1911, 18,000 white and 14,000 black timber workers in Louisiana. This is the I. W. W. type of unionism, and the employers use their newspapers to make the public believe that it stands for anarchy, violence, law-breaking and atheism, because they know that if it succeeds it will break them.

This type of unionism wants Negroes—not because its promoters love Negroes—but because they realize that they cannot win if any of the working class is left out; and after winning they cannot go back on them because they could be used as scabs to break the unions.

The A. F. of L., which claims a part of the responsibility for the East St. Louis outrage, is playing with fire. The American Negro may join hands with the American capitalist and scab them out of existence. And the editor of *The Voice* calls upon Negroes to do this. We have stood the American Federation of Labor just about long enough. Join hands with the capitalists and scab them out of existence—not in the name of scabbery, but in the name of a real organization of labor. Form your own unions (the A. C. E. is already in the field) and make a truce with your capitalist enemy until you get rid of this traitor to the cause of labor. Offer your labor to capitalism if it will agree to protect you in your right to labor—and see that it does. Then get rid of the A. F. of L.

The writer has been a member of a party which stood for the rights of labor and the principle of Industrial Unionism (the 20th century kind). He understands the labor conditions of the country and desires to see the working man win out. But his first duty, here as everywhere, is to the Negro race. And he refuses to put ahead of his race's rights a collection of diddering jackasses which can publicly palliate such atrocities as that of East St. Louis and publicly assume, as Gompers did, responsibility for it. Therefore, he issues the advice to the workers of his race to "can the A. F. of L." Since the A. F. of L. chooses to put Race before Class, let us return the compliment.

––––

Lynching: *Its Cause and Cure*

Last week we had occasion to comment on the resignation of Mr. John R. Shillady from the secretaryship of the N. A. A. C. P. Mr. Shillady's statement accompanying his resignation contains these significant words:—

"I am less confident than heretofore of the speedy success of the association's full program and of the probability of overcoming within a reasonable period the forces opposed to Negro equality by the means and methods which are within the association's power to employ."

That the N. A. A. C. P. is not likely to affect the lynchings in this land can be seen with half an eye by any one who will note that Governor J. A. Burnquist of Minnesota "is also president of the St. Paul branch of the association and one of the staunch supporters of its work"; that the Minnesota lynching of last week was one of the most cynically brutal that has occurred North or South in the last ten years, and that the association has offered and is offering to give the Governor all the assistance possible.

In most of the other cases of lynchings it is assumed that all the officials were in collusion with the forces of violence, or were at any rate in acquiescence. In the present case, however, the Governor of the State is himself a high officer of the association. Yet we venture to prophesy that no more will be done in the case of the Minnesota lynchings than in the case of lynchings further south.

This leads us to a front face consideration of the problem of lynching. Why do white men lynch black men in America? We are not dealing here with the original historical cause; nor even with its present social application. We are considering merely the efficient cause. White men lynch black men or any other men because those men's lives are unprotected either by the authorities of the commonwealth or by the victims themselves. White men lynch Negroes in America because Negroes' lives are cheap. So long as they so remain, so long will lynching remain an evil to be talked about, written about, petitioned against and slobbered over. But not all the slobber, the talk or the petitions are worth the time it takes to indulge in them, so far as the saving of a single Negro life is concerned.

What, then, is the cure? The cure follows from the nature of the cause. Let Negroes determine that their lives shall no longer be cheap; but that they will exact for them as high a price as any other element in the community under similar circumstances would exact. Let them see to it that their lives are protected and defended, if not by the State, then certainly by themselves. Then we will see the cracker stopping to take counsel with himself and to think twice before he joins a mob in whose gruesome holiday sport he himself is likely to furnish one of the casualties.

"Let Negroes help to make murder costly, for by so doing they will aid the officers of the city, State and nation in instilling respect for law and order into the minds of the worst and lowest elements of our American cities." The law of every State says explicitly that killing in defense of one's own life is strictly proper, legal and justifiable. Therefore, if Negroes determine to defend themselves from the horrible outrage of lynching they should have the support of every official and every citizen who really believes in law and order and is determined to make the law of the land stand as a living reality among the people that made it.—July, 1920.

CHAPTER III.

THE NEGRO AND THE WAR. .

[While the war lasted those of us who saw unpalatable truths were compelled to do one of two things: either tell the truth as we saw it and go to jail, or camouflage the truth that we had to tell. The present writer told the truth for the most part, in so far as it related to our race relations; but, in a few cases camouflage was safer and more effective. That camouflage, however, was never of that truckling quality which was accepted by the average American editor to such a nauseating degree. I was well aware that Woodrow Wilson's protestations of democracy were lying protestations, consciously. and deliberately designed to deceive. What, then, was my duty in the face of that fact? I chose to pretend that Woodrow Wilson meant what he said, because by so doing I could safely hold up to contempt and ridicule the undemocratic practices of his administration and the actions of his white countrymen in regard to the Negro. How this was done is shown in the first two editorials of the following chapter.]

Is Democracy Unpatriotic?

The present administration is all right. But it has its obstacles to success. As usual some of the worst of these are its injudicious "friends." For instance, there are the people who are trying their best to "queer" us in the eyes of civilized Europe. These silly souls, when Negroes ask that the principle of "Justice in War Time" be applied to Negroes as well as whites, reply, in effect that this should not be; that Negroes should not want Justice—in war time—and that any such demand on their part is "disloyalty." On the contrary, it is the fullest loyalty to the letter and spirit of the President's war-aims. To say that it isn't is to presume to accuse the President of having war-aims other than those which he has set forth in the face of Europe.

Besides, no one can deny that freedom from lynching and disfranchisement and the ending of discrimination— by the Red Cross for instance—will strengthen the hand of the administration right now by strengthening its hold on the hearts of the Negro masses and will make all Negroes—soldiers as well as civilians—more competent to give effective aid in winning the war.

Let us assume that we consent to being lynched—"during the war"—and submit tamely and with commendable weakness to being Jim-crowed and disfranchised. Very well. Will not that be the proof of our spirit and of its quality? Of course. And what you *call* that spirit won't alter its quality, will it? Now, ask all the peoples of all the world what they call a people who smilingly consent to their own degradation and destruction. They call such a people cowards—because they *are* cowards. In America we call such people "niggers."

Is anyone unpatriotic enough to pretend that "cowards" can lick "Huns"? No, this great world-task can be accomplished only by men—English men, French men, Italian men, American men. Our country needs men now more than it ever did before. And those who multiply its reserve of men are adding to its strength. That is why the true patriots who really love America and want it to win the war are asking America to change its Negroes from "niggers" into men. Surely this is a patriotic request; and any one who says that it isn't must be prepared to maintain that lynching, Jim-crow and disfranchisement are consistent with patriotism and ought to be preserved. Reading the President's proclamations in

a reverent spirit, we deny both of these monstrous conclusions; and we believe that we have on our side the President of America, the world's foremost champion of democracy who defined it as "the right of all those who submit to authority to have a VOICE in their own government"—whether it be in Germany or in Georgia. And we believe that the splendid spirit of our common country, which has buckled on its sword in support of "democracy" will support us in this reasonable contention.
—July, 1918.

———

Why Is the Red Cross?

The Red Cross, or Geneva Association, was the product of a Swiss infidel. He saw how cruel to man were those who loved God most—the Christians—and, out of his large humanity and loving kindness, he evolved an organization which should bring the charity of service to lessen the lurid horrors of Christian battlefields.

A love that rose above the love of country—the love of human kind: this was the proud principle of the Red Cross. Its nurses and its surgeons, stretcher-bearers and assistants were supposed to bring relief to those who were in pain, regardless of whether they were "friends" or "enemies." Discrimination was a word which did not exist for them: and it is not supposed to exist now even as against the wounded German aviator who has bombed a Red Cross hospital.

But, alack and alas! The splendid spirit of the Swiss infidel is seemingly too high for Christian race-prejudice to reach. Where he would not discriminate even against enemies, the American branch of his international society is discriminating against most loyal friends and willing helpers—when they are Negroes. Up to date the Ameri-

can Red Cross Society, which receives government aid
and co-operation to help win the war, cannot cite the
name of a single Negro woman as a nurse. True, it says
that it has "enrolled" some. This we refuse to believe.
But even if that were true, a nurse "enrolled" cannot
save the life of any of our soldiers in France.

The Red Cross says that it wants to win the war.
What war? A white people's war, or America's and
the world's? It this were a white people's war, as some
seem to think, colored troops from Senegal, India, Egypt,
America and the West Indies would have been kept out
of it. But they were not, and we are driven to conclude
that this is a world war. Then why doesn't the American Red Cross meet it in the spirit of the President—of
world democracy? The cry goes up for nurses to save
the lives of soldiers; yet here are thousands of Negro
nurses whom the Red Cross won't accept. They must
want to give Europe a "rotten" opinion of American
democracy. For we may be sure that these things are
known in Europe—even as our lynchings are. And anyone who would give Europe a "rotten" opinion of America
at this time is no friend of America.

The American Red Cross must be compelled to do
America's work in the spirit in which America has entered the war. There need be no biting of tongues: it
must be compelled to forego Race Prejudice. If the
N. A. A. C. P. were truly what it pretends instead of a
National Association for the Advancement of Certain
People, it would put its high-class lawyers on the job and
bring the case into the United States courts. It would
charge the American Red Cross with disloyalty to the
war-aims of America. And if it does not (in spite of
the money which it got from the "silent" protest parade
and other moneys and legal talent at its disposal) then

it will merit the name which one of its own members gave it—the National Association for the Acceptance of Color Proscription. Get busy, "friends of the colored people"! For we are not disposed to regard the camouflage of those who want nurses but do not want Negro nurses in any other light than that of Bret Harte's Truthful James:—

> Which I wish to remark—
> And my language is plain—
> That for ways that are dark
> And for tricks that are vain
> The Heathen Chinee is peculiar:
> Which the same I am free to maintain.

———

A Hint of "Our Reward"

The wisdom of our contemporary ancestors, having decided that "We Negroes must make every sacrifice to help win the war and lay aside our just demands for the present that we may win a shining place on the pages of history," it must be cold comfort to learn that the first after-the-war schoolbook of American history is out, that it is written by Reuben Gold Thwaites and Calvin Noyes Kendall, that it devotes thirty-one pages to the war and America's part in the war, and that *not one word is said of the Negro's part therein.*

Of course, sensible men should feel no surprise at this, for they will realize how little the part played by the Negro in the Civil War is known by the millions of white school children who read the school histories. Yet, if there is a spark of manhood left in the bosoms of our "white men's niggers" who sold us out during the war they must feel pained and humiliated when the flood of after-the-war school histories, of which this is the first, quietly sink the Negro's contributions (as chronicled by Mr. Emmet Scott and others) into the back waters of forgetfulness.

The times change, but we don't change with them.

The Negro at the Peace Congress

Now that they have helped to win the war against Germany, the Negro people in these United States feel the absurdity of the situation in which they find themselves. They have given lavishly of their blood and treasure. They have sent their young men overseas as soldiers, and were willing to send their young women overseas as nurses; but the innate race-prejudice of the American Red Cross prevented them. They have contributed millions of dollars to the funds of this same Red Cross and scores of millions to the four Liberty Loans; and they have done all this to help make the world "safe for democracy" even while in sixteen States of the south in which nine-tenths of them reside, they have no voice in their own government. Naturally they expect that something will have to be done to remove their civil and other disabilities. This expectation of theirs is a just and reasonable one. But——

Now that the world is getting ready for the Peace Congress which is expected to settle *the questions about which the war was fought* our Negroes want to know if the Peace Congress will settle such questions as those of lynching, disfranchisement and segregation. IT WILL NOT! And why? Simply because the war was not fought over these questions. Even a fool can see that. Lynching, disfranchisement and Jim-crowing in America are questions of American domestic policy and can be regulated only by American law-making and administrative bodies. Even a fool should be able to see this. And, since it was only by the military aid of the United States that the Allies were able to win the war, why should our people be stupid enough to think that the allied nations will aim a slap at the face of the United States (even if such things were customary) by attempting to interfere in her domestic arrangements and institutions?

We learn that various bodies of Negroes, who do not seem to understand the modern system of political government under which they live, are seeking to get money from the unsuspecting masses of our people "for the purpose of sending delegates to the Peace Congress." The project is sublimely silly. In the first place, the Peace Congress is not open to anybody who chooses to be sent. A peep into any handbook of modern history would show that Peace Congresses are made up only of delegates chosen by the heads of the governments of the countries which have been at war, and never by civic, propaganda, or other bodies within those nations. Only the President of the United States has power to designate the American delegates to the Peace Congress.

Of course, if any body of people wish to send a visitor to Versailles or Paris *at their expense,* the government of the United States has nothing to do with that and would not prevent it. But such visitor, lacking credentials from the President, could not get within a block of the Peace Congress. They can (if they read French) get from the papers published in the city where the Congress meets so much of the proceedings as the Congress may choose to give to the press. But that is all; and for that it is not necessary to go to France. Just send to France for copies of *Le Temps* or *Le Matin* and prevent a useless waste of the money of poor people who can ill afford it in any case.

"But," we are told, "such person or persons can make propaganda (in France) which will force the Peace Congress to consider American lynching, disfranchisement and segregation." Passing over the argument that such person or persons would have to be able to write French fluently, we wish to point out that the public sentiment of even one French city takes more than a month to work up; that the sentiment of one French city can have but slight weight with the Congress, and that, if it could rise to the height of embarrassing them, the French authorities would sternly put it down and banish the troublesome persons. Karl Marx, Prince Kropotkin, Malatesta and Lenine are cases in point as showing what France has done under less provoking circumstances.

Let us not try to play the part of silly fools. Lynching, disfranchisement and segregation are evils HERE; and the place in which we must fight them is HERE. If foolish would-be leaders have no plan to lay before our people for the fighting HERE, in God's name, let them say so, and stand out of the way! Let us gird up our loins for the stern tasks which lie before us HERE and address ourselves to them with courage and intelligence.

———

Africa and the Peace

"This war, disguise it how we may, is really being fought over African questions." So said Sir Harry Johnston, one of the foremost authorities on Africa, in the London Sphere in June, 1917. We wonder if the Negroes of the Western world quite · realize what this means. Wars are not fought for ideals but for lands whose populations can be put to work, for resources that can be minted into millions, for trade that can be made to enrich the privileged few. When King Leopold of Belgium

and Thomas Fortune Ryan of New York joined hands
to exploit the wealth of the Congo they did it with oiled
phrases on their lips. They called that land of horrors
and of shame "The Congo FREE State!"

And, so, when Nations go to war, they never openly
declare what they WANT. They must camouflage their
sordid greed behind some sounding phrase like "freedom
of the seas," "self-determination," "liberty" or "democracy." But only the ignorant millions ever think that
those are the real objects of their bloody rivalries. When
the war is over, the mask is dropped, and then they seek
"how best to scramble at the shearers' feast." It is then
that they disclose their real war aims.

One of the most striking cases in point is the present
peace congress. Already President Wilson has had to go
to look after democracy himself. Already responsible
heads of the Allied governments are making it known
that "freedom of the seas" means a benevolent naval
despotism maintained by them, and that "democracy"
means simply the transfer of Germany's African lands
to England and the others. Africa at the peace table constitutes the real stakes which the winners will rake in.
We may read in headlines the startling item "Negroes
Ask For German Colonies," but Negroes of sense should
not be deluded. They will not get them because they
have no battleships, no guns, no force, military or financial. They are not a Power.

Despite the pious piffle of nice old gentlemen like Professor Kelly Miller, the King-word of modern nations is
POWER. It is only Sunday school "kids" and people of
child-races who take seriously such fables as that in the
"Band of Hope Review" when we were children that
"the secret of England's greatness is the Bible." The
secret of England's greatness (as well as of any other

great nation's) is not bibles but bayonets—bayonets, business and brains. As long as the white nations have a preponderance of these, so long will they rule. Ask Japan: she knows. And as long as the lands of Africa can yield billions of business, so long will white brains use bayonets to keep them—as the British government did last year in Nigeria.

Africa is turning over in her sleep, and this agitation now going on among American Negroes for the liberation of Africa is a healthy sign of her restlessness. But it is no more than that. Africa's hands are tied, and, so tied, she will be thrown upon the peace table. Let us study how to unloose her bonds later. Instead of futile expectations from the doubtful generosity of white land-grabbers, let us American Negroes go to Africa, live among the natives and LEARN WHAT THEY HAVE TO TEACH US (for they have much to teach us). Let us go there—not in the coastlands,—but in the interior, in Nigeria and Nyassaland; let us study engineering and physics, chemistry and commerce, agriculture and industry; let us learn more of nitrates, of copper, rubber and electricity; so will we know why Belgium, France, England and Germany want to be in Africa. Let us begin by studying the scientific works of the African explorers and stop reading and believing the silly slush which ignorant missionaries put into our heads about the alleged degradation of our people in Africa. Let us learn to know Africa and Africans so well that every educated Negro will be able at a glance to put his hand on the map of Africa and tell where to find the Jolofs, Ekois, Mandingoes, Yorubas, Bechuanas or Basutos and can tell something of their marriage customs, their property laws, their agriculture and systems of worship. For, not until we can do this will it be seemly for us to pretend to be anxious about their political welfare.

Indeed, it would be well now for us to establish friendly relations and correspondence with our brothers at home. For we don't know enough about them to be able to do them any good at THIS peace congress (even if we were graciously granted seats there) ; but fifty years from now —WHO KNOWS?

"They Shall Not Pass!"

When heroic France was holding the Kaiser's legions at bay her inflexible resolution found expression in the phrase, "Ils ne passeront pas!"—they shall not pass! The white statesmen who run our government in Washington seem to have adopted the poilu's watchword in a less worthy cause. The seventy-odd Negro "delegates" to the Peace Congress who have got themselves "elected" at mass-meetings and concerts for the purpose of going to France are not going—unless they can walk, swim, or fly. For the government will not issue passports for them.

Of course, the government is not telling them so in plain English. That wouldn't be like our government. It merely makes them wait while their money melts away. Day after day and week after week, they wearily wend their way to the official Circumlocution Office where they receive a reply considered sufficient for their child-minds: "Not yet."

It is many weeks since Madam Walker, Mr. Trotter, Judge Harrison and other lesser lights were elected, but "They shall not pass!" says the government with the backing of Emmett Scott. THE VOICE holds no brief for these people: in fact it has taken the trouble to tell them more than once how silly their project was. But it is not out of order to inquire why the government will not let them go, and to find an answer to that question.

The government will not let them go to France, because the government's conscience is not clear. And the government ordered that ludicrous lackey, Mr. R. R. Moton, to go—for the same reason. In fact, the creation of sine-cures for Mr. Scott and the other barnacles is due largely to an uneasy conscience. How would it look to have Negroes telling all Europe that the land which is to make the world "safe for democracy" is rotten with race-prejudice; Jim-crows Negro officers on ships coming over from France and on trains run under government control; condones lynching by silent acquiescence and refuses to let its Negro heroes vote as citizens in that part of the country in which nine-tenths of them live. This wouldn't do at all.

Therefore: They shall not pass! And if, finally, the government, nettled by such criticisms, should lift the ban when the Peace Congress is practically over, the Negroes of America may be sure that those permitted to go will be carefully hand-picked.

But what is the matter with America as a land for pioneer work in planting democracy? Are these Negro *emigrés* afraid to face the white men here in the Republican Party or any other and raise Hades until the Constitution is enforced? Is cowardice the real reason for their running to France to uncork their mouths? It looks very much like it. Ladies and gentlemen: don't run. The fight is here, and here you will be compelled to face it, or report to us the reason why.

A Cure for the Ku-Klux

It was in the city of Pulaski in Giles County, Tennessee, that the original Ku-Klux Klan was organized in the latter part of 1865. The war had hardly been declared officially at an end when the cowardly "crackers" who couldn't lick the Yankees began organizing to take it out of the Negroes. They passed laws declaring that any black man who couldn't show three hundred dollars should be declared a vagrant; that every vagrant should be put to work in the chain-gang on the public works of their cities; that three Negroes should not gather together unless a white man was with them, and other such methods were used as were found necessary to maintain "white supremacy." When the national Congress met in December, 1865, it looked upon these light diversions with an unfriendly eye and, noting that nothing short of the re-enslavement of the Negroes would satisfy the "crackers," it kept them out of Congress until they would agree to do better. Finding that they were stiff-necked, Congress passed the 14th and 15th amendments and put the "cracker" states under military rule until they accepted the amendments. The result was that the Negro got the ballot as a protection from "the people who know him best."

In the meanwhile, the Ku-Klux after rampaging around under the leadership of that traitor, General Nathaniel B. Forrest, was put down—for good, as it was thought. Today, after the Negro has been stripped of the ballot's protection by the connivance of white Republicans in Washington and white Democrats at the South, the Ku-Klux dares to raise its ugly head in its ancestral state of Tennessee. This time they want to increase that fine brand of democracy which every coward editor knows that Negroes were getting when they were bidding them to be patriotic. The Ku-Klux means to shoot them into submission and torture them into terror before they get to showing their wounds and asking for the ballot as a recompense.

In this crisis what have the Negro "leaders" got to say on their people's behalf? Where is Emmett Scott? Where are Mr. Moton and Dr. Du Bois? What will the N. A. A. C. P. do besides writing frantic letters? We fear that they can never rise above the level of appeals. But suppose the common Negro in Tennessee decides to take a hand in the game? Suppose he lets it be known that for the life of every Negro soldier or civilian, two "crackers" will die? Suppose he lets them know that it will be as costly to kill Negroes as it would be to kill real people? Then indeed the Ku-Klux would be met upon its own ground. And why not?

All our laws, even in Tennessee, declare that lynching and white-capping are crimes against the person. All our laws declare that people singly or in groups have the right to kill in defense of their lives. And if the Ku-Klux prevents the officers of the law from enforcing that law, then it is up to Negroes to help the officers by enforcing the law on their own account. Why shouldn't they do it? Lead and steel, fire and poison are just as potent against "crackers" as they were against Germans, and democracy is as well worth fighting for in Tennessee as ever it was on the plains of France. Not until the Negroes of the south recognize this truth will anybody else recognize it for them.

"Hereditary bondmen, know ye not
Who would be free themselves must strike the blow?"

CHAPTER IV.

THE NEW POLITICS.

The New Politics for the New Negro

The world of the future will look upon the world of today as an essentially new turning point in the path of human progress. All over the world the spirit of democratic striving is making itself felt. The new issues have brought forth new ideas of freedom, politics, industry and society at large. The new Negro living in this new world is just as responsive to these new impulses as other people are.

In the "good old days" it was quite easy to tell the Negro to follow in the footsteps of those who had gone before. The mere mention of the name Lincoln or the Republican party was sufficient to secure his allegiance to that party which had seen him stripped of all political power and of civil rights without protest—effective or otherwise.

Things are different now. The new Negro is demanding elective representation in Baltimore, Chicago and other places. He is demanding it in New York. The pith of the present occasion is, that he is no longer begging or asking. He is demanding as a right that which he is in position to enforce.

In the presence of this new demand the old political leaders are bewildered, and afraid; for the old idea of Negro leadership by virtue of the white man's selection has collapsed. The new Negro leader must be chosen by his fellows—by those whose strivings he is supposed to represent.

Any man today who aspires to lead the Negro race must set squarely before his face the idea of "Race First" Just as the white men of these and other lands are white men before they are Christians, Anglo-Saxons or Republicans; so the Negroes of this and other lands are intent upon being Negroes before they are Christians, Englishmen, or Republicans.

Sauce for the goose is sauce for the gander. Charity begins at home, and our first duty is to ourselves. It is not what we wish but what we must, that we are concerned with. The world, as it ought to be, is still for us, as for others, the world that does not exist. The world as it is, is the real world, and it is to that real world that we address ourselves. Striving to be men, and finding no effective aid in government or in politics, the Negro of the Western world must follow the path of the Swadesha movement of India and the Sinn Fein movement of Ireland. The meaning of both these terms is "ourselves first." This is the mental background of the new politics of the New Negro, and we commend it to the consideration of all the political parties. For it is upon this background that we will predicate such policies as shall seem to us necessary and desirable.

In the British Parliament the Irish Home Rule party clubbed its full strength and devoted itself so exclusively to the cause of Free Ireland that it virtually dictated for a time the policies of Liberals and Conservatives alike.

The new Negro race in America will not achieve political self-respect until it is in a posiiton to organize itself as a politically independent party and follow the example of the Irish Home Rulers. This is what will happen in American politics.—September, 1917.

The Drift in Politics

The Negroes of America—those of them who think—are suspicious of everything that comes from the white people of America. They have seen that every movement for the extension of democracy here has broken down as soon as it reached the color line. Political democracy declared that "all men are created equal," meant only all white men; the Christian church found that the brotherhood of man did not include God's bastard children; the public school system proclaimed that the school house was the backbone of democracy—"for white people only," and the civil service says that Negroes must keep their place—at the bottom. So that they can hardly be blamed for looking askance at any new gospel of freedom. Freedom to them has been like one of

> "those juggling fiends
> That palter with us in a double sense;
> That keep the word of promise to our ear,
> And break it to our hope."

In this connection, some explanation of the former political solidarity of those Negroes who were voters may be of service. Up to six years ago the one great obstacle to the political progress of the colored people was their sheep-like allegiance to the Republican party. They were taught to believe that God had raised up a peculiar race of men called Republicans who had loved the slaves so tenderly that they had taken guns in their hands and rushed on the ranks of the southern slaveholders to free the slaves; that this race of men was still in existence, marching under the banner of the Republican party and showing their great love for Negroes by appointing from six to sixteen near-Negroes to soft political snaps. Today that great political superstition is falling to pieces before the advance of intelligence among Negroes. They begin to realize that they were sold out by the Republican party in 1876; that in the last twenty-five years lynchings have increased, disfranchisement has spread all over the South and "Jim-crow" cars run even into the national capitol— with the continuing consent of a Republican Congress, a Republican Supreme Court and Republican President.

Ever since the Brownsville affair, but more clearly since Taft declared and put in force the policy of pushing out the few near-Negro officeholders, the rank and file have come to see that the Republican party is a great big sham. Many went over to the Democratic party because, as the *Amsterdam News* puts it, "They had nowhere else to go." Twenty years ago the colored men who joined that party were ostracized as scalawags and crooks. But today, the defection to the Democrats of such men as Bishop Walters, Wood, Morton, Carr and Langston—whose uncle was a colored Republican Congressman from Virginia—has made the colored democracy respectable and given quite a tone to political heterdoxy.

All this loosens the bonds of their allegiance and breaks the bigotry of the last forty years. But of this change in their political view-point the white world knows nothing. The two leading Negro newspapers are subsidized by the same political pirates who own the title-deeds to the handful of hirelings holding office in the name of the Negro race. One of these papers is an organ of Mr. Washington, the other pretends to be independent—that is, it must be bought on the installment plan, and both of them are in New York. Despite this "conspiracy of silence" the Negroes are waking up, are beginning to think for themselves, to look with more favor on "new doctrines."*

Today the politician who wants the support of the Negro voter will have to give something more than pie-crust promises. The old professional "friend to the colored people" must have something more solid than the name of Lincoln and party appointments.

We demand what the Irish and the Jewish voter get: nominations on the party's ticket in our own districts. And if we don't get this we will smash the party that refuses to give it.

For we are not Republicans, Democrats or Socialists any longer. We are Negroes first. And we are no longer begging for sops. We demand, not "recognition," but representation, and we are out to throw our votes to *any* party which gives us this, and withhold them from any party which refuses to give it. No longer will we follow any leader whose job the party controls. For we know that no leader so controlled can oppose such party in our interests beyond a given point.

That is why so much interest attaches to the mass-meeting to be held at Palace Casino on the 29th where the Citizens' Committee will make its report to the Negro voters of Harlem and tell them how it was "turned down" by the local representatives of the Republican party when it begged the boon of elective representation. All such rebuffs will make for manhood—if we are men—and will drive us to play in American politics the same role which the Irish party played in British politics. That is the new trend in Negro politics, and we must not let any party forget it.—1917.

---

*The first part of this editorial is reprinted from an article written in 1912.

A Negro for President

For many years the Negro has been the football of American politics. Kicked from pillar to post, he goes begging, hat in hand, from a Republican convention to a Democratic one. Always is he asking some one else to do something for him. Always is he begging, pleading, demanding or threatening. In all these cases his dependence is on the good will, sense of justice or gratitude of the other fellow. And in none of these cases is the political reaction of the other fellow within the control of the Negro.

But a change for the better is approaching. Four years ago, the present writer was propounding in lectures, indoors and outdoors, the thesis that the Negro people of America would never amount to anything much politically until they should see fit to imitate the Irish of Britain and to organize themselves into a political party of their own whose leaders, on the basis of this large collective vote, could "hold up" Republicans, Democrats, Socialists or any other political group of American whites. As in many other cases, we have lived to see time ripen the fruits of our own thought for some one else to pluck. Here is the editor of the *Challenge* making a campaign along these very lines. His version of the idea takes the form of advocating the nomination of a Negro for the Presidency of the United States. In this form we haven't the slightest doubt that this idea will meet with a great deal of ridicule and contempt. Nevertheless, we venture to prophesy that, whether in the hands of Mr. Bridges or another, it will come to be ultimately accepted as one of the finest contributions to Negro statesmanship.

No one pretends, of course, that the votes of Negroes can elect a Negro to the high office of President of the

United States. Nor would any one expect that the votes of white people will be forthcoming to assist them in such a project. The only way in which a Negro could be elected President of the United States would be by virtue of the voters not knowing that the particular candidate was of Negro ancestry. This, we believe, has already happened within the memory of living men. But, the essential intent of this new plan is to furnish a focussing-point around which the ballots of the Negro voters may be concentrated for the realization of racial demands for justice and equality of opportunity and treatment. It would be carrying "Race First" with a vengeance into the arena of domestic politics. It would take the Negro voter out of the ranks of the Republican, Democratic and Socialist parties and would enable their leaders to trade the votes of their followers, openly and above-board, for those things for which masses of men largely exchange their votes.

Mr. Bridges will find that the idea of a Negro candidate for President presupposes the creation of a purely Negro party and upon that prerequisite he will find himself compelled to concentrate. Doubtless, most of the political wise-acres of the Negro race will argue that the idea is impossible because it antagonizes the white politicians of the various parties. They will close their eyes to the fact that politics implies antagonism and a conflict of interest. They will fail to see that the only things which count with politicians are votes, and that, just as one white man will cheerfully cut another white man's throat to get the dollars which a black man has, so will one white politician or party cut another one's throat polit-ically to get the votes which black men may cast at the polls. But these considerations will finally carry the day. Let there be no mistake. The Negro will never be accepted by the white American democracy except in so far as he can by the use of force, financial, political or other, win, seize or maintain in the teeth of opposition that position which he finds necessary to his own security and salvation. And we Negroes may as well make up our minds now that we can't depend upon the good-will of white men in anything or at any point where our interests and theirs conflict. Disguise it as we may, in business, politics, education or other departments of life, we as Negroes are compelled to fight for what we want to win from the white world.

It is easy enough for those colored men whose psychology is shaped by their white inheritance to argue the ethics of compromise and inter-racial co-operation. But we whose brains are still unbastardized must face the frank realities of this situation of racial conflict and competition. Wherefore, it is well that we marshal our forces to withstand and make head against the constant racial pressure. Action and reaction are equal and opposite. Where there is but slight pressure a slight resistance will suffice. But where, as in our case, that pressure is grinding and pitiless, the resistance that would re-establish equal conditions of freedom must of necessity be intense and radical. And it is this philosophy which must furnish the motive for such a new and radical departure as is implied in the joint idea of a Negro party in American politics and a Negro candidate for the Presidency of these United States.—June, 1920.

When the Tail Wags the Dog

Politically, these United States may be roughly divided into two sections, so far as the Negroes are concerned. In the North the Negro population has the vote. In the

South it hasn't. This was not always so. There was a time when the Negro voters of the South sent in to Congress a thin but steady stream of black men who represented their political interests directly. Due to the misadventures of the reconstruction period, this stream was shut off until at the beginning of this century George White, of North Carolina, was the sole and last representative of the black man with a ballot in the South.

This result was due largely to the characteristic stupidity of the Negro voter. He was a Republican, he was. He would do anything with his ballot for Abraham Lincoln—who was dead—but not a thing for himself and his family, who were all alive and kicking. For this the Republican party loved him so much that it permitted the Democrats to disfranchise him while it controlled Congress and the courts, the army and navy, and all the machinery of law-enforcement in the United States. With its continuing consent, Jim-crowism, disfranchisement, segregation and lynching spread abroad over the land. The end of it all was the reduction of the Negro in the South to the position of a political serf, an industrial peon and a social outcast.

Recently there has been developed in the souls of black folk a new manhood dedicated to the proposition that, if all Americans are equal in the matter of baring their breasts to foreign bayonets, then all Americans must, by their own efforts, be made equal in balloting for Presidents and other officers of the government. This principle is compelling the Republican party in certain localities to consider the necessity of nominating Negroes on its local electoral tickets. Yet the old attitude of that party on the political rights of Negroes remains substantially the same.

Here, for instance, is the Chicago convention, at which

the Negro delegates were lined up to do their duty by the party. Of course, these delegates had to deal collectively with the white leaders. This was to their mutual advantage. But the odd feature of the entire affair was this, that, *Whereas the Negro people in the South are not free to cast their votes, it was precisely from these voteless areas that the national Republican leaders selected the political spokesmen for the voting Negroes of the North.* Men who will not vote at the coming election and men who, like Roscoe Simmons, never cast a vote in their lives were the accredited representatives in whose hands lay the destiny of a million Negro voters.

But there need be no fear that this insult will annoy the black brother in the Republican ranks. A Negro Republican generally runs the rhinoceros and the elephant a close third. In plain English, the average Negro Republican is too stupid to see and too meek to mind. Then, too, here is Fate's retribution for the black man in the North who has never cared enough to fight (the Republican party) for the political freedom of his brother in the South, but left him to rot under poll-tax laws and grandfather clauses. The Northern white Democrats, for letting their Southern brethren run riot through the Constitution, must pay the penalty of being led into the ditch by the most ignorant, stupid and vicious portion of their party. Even so, the Northern Negro Republican, for letting his Southern brother remain a political ragamuffin, must now stomach the insult of this same ragamuffin dictating the destiny of the freer Negroes of the North. In both cases the tail doth wag the dog because of "the solid South." Surely, "the judgments of the Lord are true and righteous altogether!"—July, 1920.

The Grand Old Party

In the early days of 1861, when the Southern Senators and Representatives were relinquishing their seats in the United States Congress and hurling cartels of defiant explanation broadcast, the Republican party in Congress, under the leadership of Charles Francis Adams of Massachusetts, organized a joint committee made up of thirteen members of the Senate and thirty-three members of the House to make overtures to the seceding Southerners. The result of this friendly gesture was a proposed thirteenth amendment, which, if the Southerners had not been so obstinate, would have bridged the chasm. For this amendment proposed to make the slavery of the black man in America eternal and inescapable. It provided that no amendment to the Constitution, or any other proposition affecting slavery in any way, could ever be legally presented upon the floor of Congress unless its mover had secured the previous consent of *every Senator and Representative from the slave-holding States.* It put teeth into the Fugitive Slave Law and absolutely gave the Negro over into the keeping of his oppressors.

Most Negro Americans (and white ones, too) think it fashionable to maintain the most fervid faith and deepest ignorance about points in their national history of which they should be informed. We therefore submit that these facts are open and notorious to those who know American history. The record will be found slimly and shamefacedly given in McPherson's "History of the Rebellion"; at indignant length in Blaine's "Twenty Years of Congress" and Horace Greeley's "The Great American Conflict." The document can be examined in Professor Macdonald's "Select Documents of United States History." These works are to be found in every public library, and we refer to them here because there are "intellectual" Negroes today who are striving secretly, when they dare not do so openly, to perpetuate the bonds of serfdom which bind the Negro Americans to the Republican party. This bond of serfdom, this debt of gratitude, is supposed to hinge on the love which Abraham Lincoln and his party are supposed to have borne towards the Negro; and the object of this appeal to the historical record is to show that that record demonstrates that if the Negro owes any debt to the Republican party it is a debt of execration and of punishment rather than one of gratitude.

It is an astounding fact that in his First Inaugural Address Abraham Lincoln gave his explicit approval to the substance of the Crittenden resolutions which the joint committee referred to above had collectively taken over. This demonstrates that the Republican party at the very beginning of its contact with the Negro was willing to sell the Negro, bound hand and foot, for the substance of its own political control. This Thirteenth Amendment was adopted by six or eight Northern States, including Pennsylvania and Illinois; and if Fort Sumter had not been fired upon it would have become by State action the law of the land.

The Republican party did not fight for the freedom of the Negro, but for the maintenance of its own grip on the government which the election of Abraham Lincoln had secured. If any one wants to know for what the Republican party fought he will find it in such facts as this: That thousands of square miles of the people's property were given away to Wall Street magnates who had corrupted the Legislature in their effort to build railroads on the government's money. The sordid story is given in "Forty Years in Wall Street," by the banker, Henry

Clews, and others who took part in this raid upon the resources of a great but stupid people.

But the Civil War phase of the Republican party's treason to the Negro is not the only outstanding one, as was shown by the late General Tremaine in his "Sectionalism Unmasked." Not only was General Grant elected in 1868 by the newly created Negro vote, as the official records prove, but his re-election in 1872 was effected by the same means. So was the election of Rutherford B. Hayes in 1876. Yet when the election of Hayes had been taken before the overwhelmingly Republican Congress this shameless party made a deal whereby, in order to pacify the white "crackers" of the South, the Negro was given over into the hands of the triumphant Ku-Klux; the soldiers who protected their access to the ballot box in the worst southern states were withdrawn, while the "crackers" agreed as the price of this favor to withdraw their opposition to the election of Hayes. For this there exists ample proof which will be presented upon the challenge of any politician or editor. As a Republican Senator from New England shamelessly said, it was a matter of "Root, hog, or die" for the helpless Negro whose ballots had buttressed the Republican party's temple of graft and corruption. So was reconstruction settled against the Negro by the aid and abetting of the Republican party.

And since that time lynching, disfranchisement and segregation have grown with the Republican party in continuous control of the government from 1861 to 1920 —with the exception of eight years of Woodrow Wilson and eight years of Grover Cleveland. With their continuing consent the South has been made solid, so that at every Republican convention delegates who do not represent a voting constituency but a grafting collection of white postmasters and their Negro lackeys can turn the scales of nomination in favor of any person whom the central clique of the party, controlled as it has always been by Wall Street financiers, may foist upon a disgusted people, as they have done in the case of Harding. So long as the South remains solid, so long will the Republican delegates from the South consist of only this handful of hirelings; so long will they be amenable to the "discipline" which means the pressure of the jobs by which they get their bread. Therefore the Republican leaders will know that the solidarity of the South is their most valuable asset; and they are least likely to do anything that will break that solidarity. The Republican party's only interest in the Negro is to get his vote for nothing; and so long as Negro Republican leaders remain the contemptible grafters and political procurers that they are at present, so long will it get Negro votes for nothing.

Through it all the Republican party remains the most corrupt influence among Negro Americans. It buys up by jobs, appointments and gifts those Negroes who in politics should be the free and independent spokesmen of Negro Americans. But worse than this is its private work in which it secretly subsidizes men who pose before the public as independent radicals. These intellectual pimps draw private supplementary incomes from the Republican party to sell out the influence of any movement, church or newspaper with which they are connected. Of the enormity of this mode of procedure and the extent to which it saps the very springs of Negro integrity the average Negro knows nothing. Its blighting, baleful influence is known only to those who have trained ears to hear and trained eyes to see.

And now in this election the standards will advance and the cohorts go forward under the simple impulse of the same corrupting influence. But whether the new movement for a Negro party comes to a head or not, the new Negro in America will never amount to anything politically until he enfranchises himself from the Grand Old Party which has made a political joke of him.—July, 1920.

CHAPTER V.

THE PROBLEMS OF LEADERSHIP.

[In all the tangles of our awakening race consciousness there are perhaps none more knotty than the tangles relating to leadership. Leadership among Negro Americans, as among other people, means the direction of a group's activities, whether by precept, example or compulsion. But, in our case, there is involved a strikingly new element. Should the leading of our group in any sense be the product of our group's consciousness or of a consciousness originating from outside that group? What the new Negro thinks on the problem of "outside interference" in the leadership of his group is expressed in the first and sixth editorials of this chapter, one of which appeared in *The Voice* and the other in *The Negro World*.

"A Tender Point" formulates one part of the problem of leadership which is seldom touched upon by Negro Americans who characteristically avoid any public presentation of a thing about which they will talk interminably in private; namely, the claim advanced, explicitly and implicitly, by Negroids of mixed blood to be considered the natural leaders of Negro activities on the ground of some alleged "superiority" inherent in their white blood.

"The Descent of Du Bois" was written at the request of Major Loving of the Intelligence Department of the Army at the time when Dr. Du Bois, the editor of *The Crisis,* was being preened for a desk captaincy at Washington. Major Loving solicited a summary of the situation from me as one of those "radicals" qualified to furnish such a summary. This he incorporated in his report to his superiors in Washington, and this I published a week later in *The Voice* of July 25, 1918, as an editorial without changing a single word. I was informed by Major Loving that this editorial was one of the main causes of the government's change of intention as regards the Du Bois captaincy. Since that time Dr. Du Bois's white friends have been fervidly ignoring the occurrence and the consequent collapse of his leadership. "When the Blind Lead" was written as a reminder to the souls of black folks that "while it is as easy as eggs for a leader to fall off the fence, it is devilishly difficult to boost him up again."

"Just Crabs" was a delightful inspiration in the course of defending, not Mr. Garvey personally, but the principles of the New Negro Manhood Movement, a portion of which had been incorporated by him and his followers of the U. N. I. A. and A. C. L. It was the opening gun of the defense, of which some other salvos were given in the serial satire of The Crab Barrel— which I have been kind enough to omit from this record. This controversy also gave rise to the three first editorials of chapter 6.]

Our Professional "Friends"

This country of ours has produced many curious lines of endeavor, not the least curious of which is the business known as "being the Negro's friend." It was first invented by politicians, but was taken up later by "good" men, six-per-cent philanthropists, millionaire believers in "industrial education," benevolent newspapers lke the *Evening Post,* and a host of smaller fry of the "superior race." Just at this time the business is being worked to death, and we wish to contribute our mite toward the killing—by showing what it means.

The first great "friend" of the Negro was the Southern politician, Henry Clay, who, in the first half of the nineteenth century organized the American Colonization Society. This society befriended the "free men of color" by raising funds to ship them away to Liberia, whch was accepted by many free Negroes as a high proof of the white man's "friendship." But Frederick Douglass, William Still, James McCune Smith, Martin R. Delaney, and other wide-awake Negroes were able to show (by transcripts of its proceedings) that its real purpose was to get rid of the free Negroes because, so long as they continued to live here, their freedom was an inducement to the slaves to run away from slavery, and their accomplishments demonstrated to all white people that the Negro (contrary to the claims of the slave-holders) was capable of a higher human destiny than that of being chattels—and this was helping to make American slavery odious in the eyes of the civilized world.

Since that time the dismal farce of "friendship" has been played many times, by politicians, millionaires and their editorial adherents, who have been profuse in giving good advice to the Negro people. They have advised them to "go slow," that "Rome was not built in a day," and that "half a loaf is better than no bread," that "respect could not be demanded," and, in a thousand different ways have advised them that if they would only follow the counsels of "the good white people" who really had their interests at heart, instead of following their own counsels (as the Irish and the Jews do), all would yet be well. Many Negroes who have a wish-bone where their back-bone ought to be have been doing this. It was as a representative of this class that Mitchell's man, Mr. Fred R. Moore, the editor of *The Age,* spoke, when in July he gave utterance to the owlish reflection that,

The Negro race is afflicted with many individuals whose wagging tongues are apt to lead them into indiscreet utterances that reflect upon the whole race. . . . The unruly tongues should not be allowed to alienate public sympathy from the cause of the oppressed.

It was as a fairly good representative of the class of "good white friends of the colored people" that Miss Mary White Ovington, the chairman of the New York Branch of the National Association for the Advancement of Colored People, sent to *The Voice* the following bossy and dictatorial note:

My dear Mr. Harrison,
    I don't see any reason for another organization, or another paper. If you printed straight socialism it might be different.
Yours truly,
MARY W. OVINGTON.

These "good white people" must really forgive us for insisting that we are not children, and that, while we want all the friends we can get, we need no benevolent dictators. It is we, and not they, who must shape Negro policies. If they want to help in carrying them out we will appreciate their help.

Just now the white people—even in the South—have felt the pressure of the new Negro's manhood demands, in spite of the fact that backward-looking Negroes like *The Age's* editor condemn the inflexible spirit of these demands. All over the South, the white papers, scared by the exodus of Negro laborers who are tired of begging for justice overdue, are saying that we are right, and friendlier legislation has begun to appear on Southern statute books. Mr. Mencken and other Southern writers are saying that the Negro is demanding, and that the South had better accede to his just demands, as it is only a matter of time when he will be in position to enforce them. One should think, then, that those who have been parading as our professional friends would be in the van of this manhood movement. But the movement seems to have left them in the rear. Now, that we are demanding the whole loaf, they are begging for half, and are angry at us for going further than they think "nice."

It was the N. A. A. C. P. which was urging us to compromise our manhood by begging eagerly for "Jim Crow" training camps. And the same group is asking, in the November *Crisis*, that we put a collective power-of-attorney into their hands and leave it to them to shape our national destiny. The N. A. A. C. P. has done much good work for Negroes—splendid work—in fighting lynching and segregation. For that we owe it more gratitude and good will than we owe to the entire Republican party for the last sixty years of its existence. But we cannot, even in this case, abdicate our right to shape more radical policies for ourselves. It was the realization of the need for a more radical policy than that of the N. A. A. C. P. that called into being the Liberty League of Negro Americans. And the N. A. A. C. P., as mother, must forgive its offspring for forging farther ahead.

Then, there is the case of the New York *Evening Post*, of which Mr. Villard is owner. This paper was known far and wide as "a friend to Negroes." But its friendship has given way to indifference and worse. In the good old days every lynching received editorial condemnation. But the three great lynchings this year which preceded East St. Louis found no editorial of condemnation in the *Post*. It was more than luke-warm then. But, alack and alas! As soon as the Negro soldiers in Houston, goaded to retaliation by gross indignities, did some shooting on their own account, the *Evening Post*, which had no condemnation of the conduct of the lynchers, joined the chorus of those who were screaming for "punishment" and death. Here is its brief editorial on August 25th:

As no provocation could justify the crimes committed by mutinous Negro soldiers at Houston, Texas, so no condemnation of their conduct can be too severe. It may be that the local authorities were not wholly blameless, and that the commanding officers were at fault in not foreseeing the trouble and taking steps to guard against it. But nothing can really palliate the offence of the soldiers. They were false to their uniform; they were false to their race. In one sense, this is the most deplorable aspect of the whole riotous outbreak. It will play straight into the hands of men like Senator Vardaman who have been saying that it was dangerous to draft colored men into the army. And the feeling against having colored troops encamped in the South will be intensified. The grievous harm which they might do to their own people should have been all along in the minds of the colored soldiers, and made them doubly circumspect. They were under special obligation, in addition to their military oath, to conduct themselves so as not to bring reproach upon the Negroes as a whole, of whom they were in a sort representative. Their criminal outrage will tend to make people forget the good work done by other Negro soldiers. After the rigid investigation which the War Department has ordered, the men found guilty should receive the severest punishment. As for the general army policy affecting colored troops, we are glad to see that Secretary Baker appears to intend no change in his recent orders.

We ourselves cannot forget that while the question of whether the *Post's* editor would get a diplomatic appointment (like some other editors) was under consideration during the first year of Woodrow Wilson's first administration, the *Post* pretended to believe that the President didn't know of the segregation practiced in the government departments. The N. A. A. C. P., whose letter sent out at the time is now before us, pretended to the same effect.

After viewing these expressions of frightful friendliness in our own times, we have reached the conclusion that the time has come when we should insist on being our own best friends. We may make mistakes, of course, but we ought to be allowed to make our own mistakes— as other people are allowed to do. If friendship is to mean compulsory compromise foisted on us by kindly white people, or by cultured Negroes whose ideal is the imitation of the urbane acquiescence of these white friends, then we had better learn to look a gift horse in the mouth whenever we get the chance.—November, 1917.

Shillady Resigns

Mr. John R. Shillady, ex-secretary of the N. A. A. C. P., states in his letter of resignation that "I am less confident than heretofore of the speedy success of the association's full program and of the probability of overcoming within a reasonable period the forces opposed to Negro equality by the means and methods which are within the association's power to employ." In this one sentence Mr. Shillady, the worker on the inside, puts in suave and serenely diplomatic phrase the truth which people on the outside have long ago perceived, namely, that the N. A. A. C. P. makes a joke of itself when it affects to think that lynching and the other evils which beset the Negro in the South can be abolished by simple publicity. The great weakness of the National Association for the Advancement of Colored People has been and is that, whereas it aims to secure certain results by affecting the minds of white people and making them friendly to it, it has no control over these minds and has absolutely no answer to the question, "What steps do you propose to take if these minds at which you are aiming remain unaffected? What do you propose to do to secure life and liberty for the Negro if the white Southerner persists, as he has persisted for sixty years, in refusing to grant guarantees of life and liberty?" The N. A. A. C. P. has done some good and worth-while work as an organization of protest. But the times call for something more effective than protests addressed to the other fellow's consciousness. What is needed at present is more of the mobilizing of the Negro's political power, pocketbook power and intellectual power (which are absolutely within the Negro's own control) to do for the Negro the things which the Negro needs to have done without depending upon or waiting for the co-operative action of white people. This co-operative action, whenever it does come, is a boon that no Negro, intelligent or unintelligent, affects to despise. But no Negro of clear vision, whether he be a leader or not, can afford to predicate the progress of the Negro upon such co-operative action, because it may not come.

Mr. Shillady may have seen these things. It is high time that all Negroes see these things whether their white professional friends see them or not.—July, 1920.

Our White Friends

In the good old days when the black man's highest value in the white man's eye was that of an object of benevolence especially provided by the Divine mind for calling out those tender out-pourings of charity which were so dear to the self-satisfied Caucasian—in those days the white men who fraternized with black people could do so as their guides, philosophers and friends without incurring any hostility on the part of black folk. Today, however, the white man who mixes with the black brother is having a hard time of it. Somehow Ham's offspring no longer feels proud of being "taken up" by the progeny of Japhet. And when the white man insists on mixing in with him the colored brother will persist in attributing ulterior motives.

What is the cause of this difference? The answer will be found only by one who refuses to wear the parochial blinkers of Anglo-Saxon civilization and sees that the relations of the white and black race have changed and are changing all over the world. Such an observer would note that the most significant fact of the growing race consciousness is to be found in the inevitable second half of the word. It isn't because these darker people are motivated by race that their present state of mind constitutes a danger to Caucasian overlordship. It is because they have developed consciousness, intelligence, understanding. They have learned that the white brother is perfectly willing to love them—"in their place." They have learned that that place is one in which they are not to develop brains and initiative, but must furnish the brawn and muscle whereby the white man's brain and initiative can take eternally the products of their brawn and muscle. There are today many white men who will befriend the Negro, who will give their dollars to his comfort and welfare, so long as the idea of what constitutes that comfort and welfare comes entirely from the white man's mind. Examples like those of Dr. Spingarn and Mr. E. D. Morel are numerous.

And not for nothing does the black man balk at the white man's "mixing in." For there are spies everywhere and the *agent provocateur* is abroad in the land. From Chicago comes the news by way of the Associated Press (white) that Dr. Jonas, who has always insisted in sticking his nose into the Negro peoples' affairs as their guide, philosopher and friend, has been forced to confess that he is a government agent, presumably paid for things which the government would later suppress. Dr. Jonas is reported to have said that he is connected with the British secret service; but since the second year of the European war it has been rather difficult for us poor devils to tell where the American government ended and the British government began, especially in these matters. In any case, we have Dr. Jonas' confession, and all the silly Negroes who listened approvingly to the senseless allegations made by Messrs. Jonas, Gabriel and others of a standing army of 4,000,000 in Abyssinia and of Japanese-Abyssinian diplomatic relations and intentions, must feel now very foolish about the final result.

How natural it was that Jonas, the white leader, should have gone scot free, while Redding and his other Negro dupes are held! How natural that Jonas should be the one to positively identify Redding as the slayer of the Negro policeman! And so, once again, that section of the Negro race that will not follow except where a white man leads will have to pay that stern penalty whereby Dame Experience teaches her dunces. Under the present circumstances we, the Negroes of the Western world, do pledge our allegiance to leaders of our own race, selected by our own group and supported financially and otherwise exclusively by us. Their leadership may be wise or otherwise; they may make mistakes here and there; nevertheless, such sins as they may commit will be our sins, and all the glory that they may achieve will be our glory. We prefer it so. It may be worth the while of the white men who desire to be "Our Professional Friends" to take note of this preference.

A Tender Point

When the convention of turtles assembled on the Grand Banks of Newfoundland it was found absolutely impossible to get a tortoise elected as leader. All turtles, conservative and radical, agreed that a land and water creature, who was half one thing and half another, was not an ideal choice for leader of a group which lived exclu-

sively in the water. Whenever a leader of the Irish has
to be selected by the Irish it is an Irishman who is selected.
No Irishman would be inclined to dispute the fact that
other men, even Englishmen like John Stuart Mill and the
late Keir Hardie, could feel the woes of Ireland as pro-
foundly as any Irishman. But they prefer to live up to the
principle of "Safety First."

These two illustrations are to be taken as a prelude to
an important point which is not often discussed in the
Negro press because all of us—black, brown and parti-
colored—fear to offend each other. That point concerns
the biological breed of persons who should be selected
by Negroes as leaders of their race. We risk the offense
this time because efficiency in matters of racial leadership,
as in other matters, should not be too tender to these
points of prejudice when they stand in the way of desirable results. For two centuries in America we, the de-
scendants of the black Negroes of Africa, have been ·
told by white men that we cannot and will not amount
to anything except in so far as we first accept the bar
sinister of their mixing with us. Always when white people had to select a leader for Negroes they would select
some one who had in his veins the blood of the selectors.
In the good old days when slavery was in flower, it was
those whom Denmark Vesey of Charleston described as
"house niggers" who got the master's cast-off clothes,
the better scraps of food and culture which fell from
the white man's table, who were looked upon as the
Talented Tenth of the Negro race. The opportunities of
self-improvement, in so far as they lay within the hand of
the white race, were accorded exclusively to this class of
people who were the left-handed progeny of the white
masters.

Out of this grew a certain attitude on their part

towards the rest of the Negro people which, unfortunately, has not yet been outgrown. In Washington, Boston, Charleston, New York and Chicago these proponents of the lily-white idea are prone to erect around their sacred personalities a high wall of caste, based on the ground of color. And the black Negroes have heretofore worshipped at the altars erected on these walls. One sees this in the Baptist, Methodist and Episcopal churches, at the various conventions and in fraternal organizations. Black people themselves seem to hold the degrading view that a man who is but half a Negro is twice as worthy of their respect and support as one who is entirely black. We have seen in the social life of some of the places mentioned how women, undeniably black and undeniably beautiful, have been shunned and ostracised at public functions by men who should be presumed to know better. We have read the fervid jeremiads of "colored" men who, when addressing the whites on behalf of some privilege which they wished to share with them, would be, in words, as black as the ace of spades, but, when it came to mixing with "their kind," they were professional lily-whites, and we have often had to point out to them that there is no color prejudice in America—except among "colored" people. Those who may be inclined to be angry at the broaching of this subject are respectfully requested to ponder that pungent fact.

In this matter white people, even in America, are inclined to be more liberal than colored people. If a white man has no race prejudice, it will be found that he doesn't care how black is the Negro friend that he takes to his home and his bosom. Even these white people who pick leaders for Negroes have begun in these latter years to give formal and official expression to this principle. Thus it was that when the trustees of Tuskegee had to elect

a head of Tuskegee and a putative leader of the Negroes
of America to succeed the late Dr. Washington, they
argued that it was now necessary to select as leader for
the Negro people a man who could not be mistaken by any
one for anything other than a Negro. Therefore, Mr.
Emmett Scott was passed over and Dr. Robert R. Morton
was selected. We are not approving here the results of
that selection, but merely holding up to Negroes the principle by which it was governed.

So long as we ourselves acquiesce in the selection of
leaders on the ground of their unlikeness to our racial
type, just so long will we be met by the invincible argument that white blood is necessary to make a Negro worth
while. Every Negro who has respect for himself and for
his race will feel, when contemplating such examples as
Toussaint Louverture, Phyllis Wheatley, Paul Laurence
Dunbar and Samuel Ringgold Ward, the thrill of
pride that differs in quality and intensity from
the feeling which he experiences when contemplating
other examples of great Negroes who are not entirely
black. For it is impossible in such cases for the white
men to argue that they owed their greatness or their
prominence to the blood of the white race which was
mingled in their veins. It is a legitimate thrill of pride,
for it gives us a hope nobler than the hope of amalgama-
tion whereby, in order to become men, we must lose our
racial identity. It is a subject for sober and serious reflection, and it is hoped that sober and serious reflection
will be given to it.

The Descent of Du Bois

In a recent bulletin of the War Department it was
declared that "justifiable grievances" were producing and

had produced "not disloyalty, but an amount of unrest and bitterness which even the best efforts of their leaders may not be able always to guide." This is the simple truth. The essence of the present situation lies in the fact that the people whom our white masters have "recognized" as our leaders (without taking the trouble to consult us) and those who, by our own selection, had actually attained to leadership among us are being re-valuated and, in most cases, rejected.

The most striking instance from the latter class is Dr. W. E. Du Bois, the editor of the *Crisis*. Du Bois's case is the more significant because his former services to his race have been undoubtedly of a high and courageous sort. Moreover, the act by which he has brought upon himself the stormy outburst of disapproval from his race is one which of itself, would seem to merit no such stern condemnation. To properly gauge the value and merit of this disapproval one must view it in the light of its attendant circumstances and of the situation in which it arose.

Dr. Du Bois first palpably sinned in his editorial "Close Ranks" in the July number of the *Crisis*. But this offense (apart from the trend and general tenor of the brief editorial) lies in a single sentence: "Let us, while this war lasts, *forget our special grievances* and close our ranks, shoulder to shoulder with our white fellow-citizens and the allied nations that are fighting for democracy." From the latter part of the sentence there is no dissent, so far as we know. The offense lies in that part of the sentence which ends with the italicized words. It is felt by all his critics, that Du Bois, of all Negroes, knows best that our "special grievances" which the War Department Bulletin describes as "justifiable" consist of lynching, segregation and disfranchisement, and that the Negroes of America can not preserve either their lives, their manhood or their vote (which is their political life and liberties) with these things in existence. The doctor's critics feel that America can not use the Negro people to any good effect unless they have life, liberty and manhood assured and guaranteed to them. Therefore, instead of the war for democracy making these things less necessary, it makes them more so.

"But," it may be asked, "why should not these few words be taken merely as a slip of the pen or a venial error in logic? Why all this hubbub?" It is because the so-called leaders of the first-mentioned class have already established an unsavory reputation by advocating this same surrender of life, liberty and manhood, masking their cowardice behind the pillars of war-time sacrifice? Du Bois's statement, then, is believed to mark his entrance into that class, and is accepted as a "surrender" of the principles which brought him into prominence—and which alone kept him there.

Later, when it was learned that Du Bois was being preened for a berth in the War Department as a captain-assistant (adjutant) to Major Spingarn, the words used by him in the editorial acquired a darker and more sinister significance. The two things fitted too well together as motive and self-interest.

For these reasons Du Bois is regarded much in the same way as a knight in the middle ages who had had his armor stripped from him, his arms reversed and his spurs hacked off. This ruins him as an influential person among Negroes at this time, alike whether he becomes a captain or remains an editor.

But the case has its roots much farther back than the editorial in July's *Crisis*. Some time ago when it was learned that the *Crisis* was being investigated by the government for an alleged seditious utterance a great clamor went up, although the expression of it was not open. Negroes who dared to express their thoughts seemed to think the action tantamount to a declaration that protests against lynching, segregation and disfranchisement were outlawed by the government. But nothing was clearly understood until the conference of editors was called under the assumed auspices of Emmet Scott and Major Spingarn. Then it began to appear that these editors had not been called without a purpose. The desperate ambiguity of the language which they used in their report (in the War Department Bulletin), coupled with the fact that not one of them, upon his return would tell the people anything of the proceedings of the conference—all this made the Negroes feel less and less confidence in them and their leadership; made them (as leaders) less effective instruments for the influential control of the race's state of mind.

Now Du Bois was one of the most prominent of those editors "who were called." The responsibility, therefore, for a course of counsel which stresses the servile virtues of acquiescence and subservience falls squarely on his shoulders. The offer of a captaincy and Du Bois's flirtation with that offer following on the heels of these things seemed, even in the eyes of his associate members of the N. A. A. C. P. to afford clear proof of that which was only a suspicion before, viz: that the racial resolution of the leaders had been tampered with, and that Du Bois had been privy to something of the sort. The connection between the successive acts of the drama (May, June, July) was too clear to admit of any interpretation other than that of deliberate, cold-blooded, purposive planning. And the connection with Spingarn seemed to suggest that personal friendships and public faith were not good working team-mates.

For the sake of the larger usefulness of Dr. Du Bois we hope he will be able to show that he can remain as editor of the *Crisis;* but we fear that it will require a good deal of explaining. For, our leaders, like Caesar's wife, must be above suspicion.—July, 1918.

When the Blind Lead

In the February issue of the Crisis its editor begins a brief editorial on "Leadership," with the touching reminder that "Many a good cause has been killed by suspected leadership." How strikingly do these words bring back to us Negroes those dark days of 1918! At that time the editor of the Crisis was offering certain unique formulas of leadership that somehow didn't "take." His "Close Ranks" editorial and the subsequent slump in the stock of his leadership have again illustrated the truth long since expressed in Latin: "Descensus Averni facilis; sed revocare gradus,—hoc opus est," which, being translated, might mean that, while it's as easy as eggs for a leader to fall off the fence, it is devilishly difficult to boost him up again. In September, 1918, one could boldly say, "The Crisis says, *first* your Country, *then* your Rights!" Today, when the Negro people everywhere are responding to Mr. Michael Coulsen's sentiment that "it's Race, not Country, first," we find the "leader" of 1918 in the position described by Lowell in these words: "A moultin' fallen cherubim, ef he should see ye'd snicker, Thinkin' he warn't a suckemstance."

How fast time flies!

But the gist of Dr. Du Bois's editorial is the moral downfall of another great leader. "Woodrow Wilson, in

following a great ideal of world unity, forgot all his
pledges to the German people, forgot all his large words
to Russia, did not hesitate to betray Gompers and his
unions, *and never at any single moment meant to include
in his democracy twelve million of his fellow Americans,
whom he categorically promised 'more than mere grudging
justice,' and then allowed 350 of them to be lynched during his Presidency.* Under such leadership what cause
could succeed?" He notes that out of the World War,
with the Allies triumphant, have come Britain's brutal
domination of the seas, her conquest of Persia, Arabia
and Egypt, and her tremendous tyranny imposed on two-
thirds of Africa.

But we saw these things, as early as 1917, to be the
necessary conquences of the Allies' success, when the
editor of the *Crisis* was telling his race: "You are not
fighting simply for Europe; you are fighting for the
world." Was Dr. Du Bois so blind then that he couldn't
see them? And if he was, is he any less blind today? In
1918 the lynchings were still going on while Dr. Du Bois
was solemnly advising us to "forget our grievances." Any
one who insisted then on putting such grievances as
lynchings, disfranchisement and segregation in the fore-
ground was described by the *Crisis'* editor as seeking "to
turn his country's tragic predicament to his own personal
gain." At that time he either believed or pretended to
believe every one of the empty words that flowed from
Woodrow Wilson's lips, and on the basis of this belief
he was willing to act as a brilliant bellwether to the rest
of the flock. Unfortunately, the flock refused to follow
the lost leader.

"If the blind lead the blind they will both fall into the
ditch." But in this case those being led were not quite so
blind as those who wanted to lead them by way of cap-

taincies in the army. Which was why some captaincies were not forthcoming. The test of vision in a leader is the ability to foresee the immediate future, the necessary consequences of a course of conduct and the dependable sentiments of those whom he assumes to lead. In all these things Dr. Du Bois has failed; and neither his ungrateful attack on Emmett Scott nor his belated discovery of Wilsonian hypocrisy will, we fear, enable him to climb back into the saddle of race leadership. This is a pity, because he has rendered good service in his day. But that day is past. The magazine which he edits still remains as a splendid example of Negro journalism. But the personal primacy of its editor has departed, never to return. Other times, other men; other men, other manners.

Even the Negro people are now insisting that their leaders shall in thought and moral stamina keep ahead of, and not behind, them.

"It takes a mind like Willum's [fact!] ez big as all out-
          doors
To find out thet it looks like rain arter it fairly pours."

The people's spiritual appetite has changed and they are no longer enamoured of "brilliant" leaders, whose chorus is:

"A marciful Providence fashioned us holler
   O' purpose that we might our principles swaller;
   It can hold any quantity on 'em—the belly can—
   An' bring 'em up ready fer use like the pelican."

And this is a change which we commend to the kindly consideration of all those good white friends who are out selecting Negro "leaders." It is a fact which, when carefully considered, will save them thousands of dollars in "overhead expense." The Negro leaders of the future will be expected not only to begin straight, take a moral vacation, and then go straight again. They will be expected to go straight all the time; to stand by us in war as well as in peace; not to blow hot and cold with the same mouth, but "to stand four-square to *all* the winds that blow."—1920.

———

Just Crabs

Once upon a time a Greedy Person went rummaging along the lagoon with a basket and a stick in quest of Crabs, which he needed for the Home Market. (Now, this was in the Beginning of Things, Best Beloved.) These were Land Crabs—which, you know, are more luscious than Sea Crabs, being more Primitive and more full of meat. He dug into their holes with his stick, routed them out, packed them on their backs in his basket and took them home. Several trips he made with his basket and his stick, and all the Crabs which he caught were dumped into a huge barrel. (But this time he didn't pack them on their backs.) And all the creatures stood around and watched. For this Greedy Person had put no cover on the barrel. (But this was in the Beginning of Things.)

He knew Crab Nature, and was not at all worried about his Crabs. For as soon as any one Crab began to climb up on the side of the barrel to work his way toward the top the other Crabs would reach up, grab him by the legs, and down he would come, kerplunk! "If we can't get up," they would say—"if we can't get up, you shan't get up, either. We'll pull you down. Besides, you should wait until the barrel bursts. There are Kind Friends on the Outside who will burst the barrel if we only wait, and then, when the Great Day dawns, we will all be Emancipated and there'll be no need for Climbing. Come down, you fool!" (Because this was in the Beginning of Things, Best Beloved.) So the Greedy Person could always get as many Crabs as he needed for the Home Market, because they all depended on him for their food.

And all the creatures stood around and laughed. For this was very funny in the Beginning of Things. And all the creatures said that the Reason for this kink in Crab Nature was that when the Creator was giving out heads he didn't have enough to go around, so the poor Crabs didn't get any. And the Greedy Person thanked his lucky stars that Crabs had been made in that Peculiar way, since it made it unnecessary to put a cover on his barrel or to waste his precious time a-watching of them. (Now, all this happened long ago, Best Beloved, in the very Beginning of Things.)

———

The above is the first of our Just-So Stories—with no apologies to Rudyard Kipling or any one else. We print it here because, just at this time the Crabs are at work in Harlem, and there is a tremendous clashing of claws as the Pull 'Em Down program goes forward. It's a great game, to be sure, but it doesn't seem to get them or us anywhere. The new day that has dawned for the Negroes of Harlem is a day of business accomplishment. People are going into business, saving their money and collectively putting it into enterprises which will mean roofs over their heads and an economic future for themselves and their little ones.

But the Subsidized Sixth are sure that this is all wrong and that we have no right to move an inch until the Socialist millennium dawns, when we will all get "out of the barrel" together. It does not seem to have occurred to them that making an imperfect heaven now does not unfit any one for enjoying the perfect paradise which they promise us—if it ever comes. Truly it is said of them, that "the power over a man's subsistence is the power over his will"—and over his "scientific radicalism," too. But we remember having translated this long ago into the less showy English of "Show me whose bread you eat, and I'll tell you whose songs you'll sing." Surely this applies to radicals overnight as well as to ordinary folk. And if not, why not?

But when the reek of the poison gas propaganda has cleared away and the smoke of the barrage has lifted it will be found that "White Men's Niggers" is a phrase that need not be restricted to old-line politicians and editors. Criticism pungent and insistent is due to every man in public life and to every movement which bids for public support. But the cowardly insinuator who from the safe shelter of nameless charges launches his poisoned arrows at other people's reputation is a contemptible character to have on any side of any movement. He is generally a liar who fears that he will be called to account for his lies if he should venture to name his foe. No man with the truth to tell indulges in this pastime of the skulker and the skunk. Let us, by all means, have clear, hard-hitting criticism, but none of this foul filth which lowers the thing that throws it. In the name of common sense and common decency, quit being Just Crabs.

CHAPTER VI.

THE NEW RACE-CONSCIOUSNESS

The Negro's Own Radicalism

Twenty years ago all Negroes known to the white publicists of America could be classed as conservatives on all the great questions on which thinkers differ. In matters of industry, commerce, politics, religion, they could be trusted to take the backward view. Only on the question of the Negro's "rights" could a small handful be found bold enough to be tagged as "radicals"—and they were howled down by both the white and colored adherents of the conservative point of view. Today Negroes differ on all those great questions on which white thinkers differ, and there are Negro radicals of every imaginary stripe—agnostics, atheists, I. W. W.'s Socialists, Single Taxers, and even Bolshevists.

In the good old days white people derived their knowledge of what Negroes were doing from those Negroes who were nearest to them, generally their own selected exponents of Negro activity or of their white point of view. A classic illustration of this kind of knowledge was afforded by the Republican Party; but the Episcopal Church, the Urban League, or the U. S. Government would serve as well. Today the white world is vaguely, but disquietingly, aware that Negroes are awake, different and perplexingly uncertain. Yet the white world by which they are surrounded retains its traditional method of interpreting the mass by the Negro nearest to themselves in affiliation or contact. The Socialist party thinks that the "unrest" now apparent in the Negro masses is due to the propaganda which its adherents support, and believes that it will function largely along the lines of socialist political thought. The great dailies, concerned mainly with their chosen task of being the mental bell-wethers of the mob, scream "Bolshevist propaganda" and flatter themselves that they have found the true cause; while the government's unreliable agents envisage it as "disloyalty." The truth, as usual, is to be found in the depths; but there they are all prevented from going by mental laziness and that traditional off-handed, easy contempt with which white men in America, from scholars like Lester Ward to scavengers like Stevenson, deign to consider the colored population of twelve millions.

In the first place, the cause of "radicalism" among American Negroes is international. But it is necessary to draw clear distinctions at the outset. The function of the Christian church is international. So is art, war, the family, rum and the exploitation of labor. But none of these is entitled to extend the mantle of its own peculiar "internationalism" to cover the present case of the Negro discontent—although this has been attempted. The international Fact to which Negroes in America are now reacting is not the exploitation of laborers by capitalists; but the social, political and economic subjection of colored peoples by white. It is not the Class Line, but the Color Line, which is the incorrect but accepted expression for the Dead Line of racial inferiority. This fact is a fact of Negro consciousness as well as a fact of externals. The international Color Line is the practice and theory of that doctrine which holds that the best stocks of Africa, China, Egypt and the West Indies are inferior to the worst stocks of Belgium, England and Italy, and must hold their lives, lands and liberties upon such terms and conditions as the white races may choose to grant them.

On the part of the whites, the motive was originally economic; but it is no longer purely so. All the available facts go to prove that, whether in the United States or in Africa or China, the economic subjection is without exception keener and more brutal when the exploited are black, brown and yellow, than when they are white. And the fact that black, brown and yellow also exploit each other brutally whenever Capitalism has created the economic classes of plutocrat and proletarian should suffice to put purely economic subjection out of court as the prime cause of racial unrest. For the similarity of suffering has produced in all lands where whites rule colored races a certain similarity of sentiment, viz.: a racial revulsion of racial feeling. The peoples of those lands begin to feel and realize that they are so subjected because they are members of races condemned as "inferior" by their Caucasian overlords. The fact presented to their minds is one of race, and in terms of race do they react to it. Put the case to any Negro by way of test and the answer will make this clear.

The great World War, by virtue of its great advertising campaign for democracy and the promises which were held out to all subject peoples, fertilized the Race Consciousness of the Negro people into the stage of conflict with the dominant white idea of the Color Line. They took democracy at its face value—which is—equality. So did the Hindus, Egyptians and West Indians. This is what the hypocritical advertisers of democracy had not bargained for. The American Negroes, like the other darker peoples, are presenting their checques and trying to "cash in," and delays in that process, however unavoidable to the paying tellers, are bound to beget a plentiful

lack of belief in either their intention or their ability to
pay. Hence the run on Democracy's bank—"the Negro
unrest" of the newspaper paragraphers.

Undoubtedly some of these newly-awakened Negroes
will take to Socialism and Bolshevism. But here again
the reason is racial. Since they suffer racially from the
world as at present organized by the white race, some of
their ablest hold that it is "good play" to encourage and
give aid to every subversive movement within that white
world which makes for its destruction "as it is." For by
its subversion they have much to gain and nothing to lose.
Yet they build on their own foundations. Parallel with
the dogma of Class-Consciousness they run the dogma of
Race-Consciousness. And they dig deeper. For the roots
of Class-Consciousness inhere in a temporary economic
order; whereas the roots of Race-Consciousness must of
necessity survive any and all changes in the economic
order. Accepting biology as a fact, their view is the
more fundamental. At any rate, it is that view with
which the white world will have to deal.—The *New
Negro,* October, 1919.

Race First Versus Class First

"In the old days white people derived their knowledge
of what Negroes were doing from those Negroes who
were nearest to them, largely their own selected exponents of Negro activity or of their white point of
view. * * * Today the white world is vaguely, but
disquietingly, aware that Negroes are awake; different,
but perplexingly uncertain. Yet the white world by which
they are surrounded retains its traditional method of interpreting the mass by the Negro nearest to themselves in
affiliation or contact. The Socialist party still persists

in thinking that the unrest now apparent in the Negro masses is due to the propaganda which its paid adherents support, and believes that the unrest will function largely along the lines of Socialist political thought."

It is necessary to insist on this point today when the Socialist party of America has secretly subsidized both a magazine and a newspaper to attempt to cut into the splendid solidarity which Negroes are achieving in response to the call of racial necessity. It is necessary to point out that "radical" young Negroes may betray the interests of the race into alien hands just as surely as "the old crowd." For, after all, the essence of both betrayals consists in making the racial requirements play second fiddle to the requirements dictated as best for it by other groups with other interests to serve. The fact that one group of alien interests is described as "radical" and the other as "reactionary" is of very slight value to us.

In the days when the Socialist Party of America was respectable, although it never drew lines of racial separation in the North, it permitted those lines to be drawn in the South. It had no word of official condemnation for the Socialists of Tennessee who prevented Theresa Malkiel in 1912 from lecturing to Negroes on Socialism either in the same hall with them or in meetings of their own. It was the national office of the party which in that same presidential year refused to route Eugene V. Debs in the South because that Grand Old Man let it be known that he would not remain silent on the race question while in the South. They wanted the votes of the white South then, and were willing to betray by silence the principles of inter-racial solidarity which they espoused on paper.

Now, when their party has shrunk considerably in popular support and sentiment, they are willing to take up our cause. Well, we thank honest white people everywhere who take up our cause, but we wish them to know that we have already taken it up ourselves. While they were refusing to diagnose our case we diagnosed it ourselves, and, now that we have prescribed the remedy—Race Solidarity—they come to us with their prescription—Class Solidarity. It is too late, gentlemen! This racial alignment is all our own product, and we have no desire to turn it over to you at this late day, when we are beginning to reap its benefits. And if you are simple enough to believe that those among us who serve your interests ahead of ours have any monopoly of intellect or information along the lines of modern learning, then you are the greater gulls indeed.

We can respect the Socialists of Scandinavia, France, Germany or England on their record. But your record so far does not entitle you to the respect of those of us who can see all around a subject. We say Race First, because you have all along insisted on Race First and class after when you didn't need our help. We reproduce below a brief portion of your record in those piping times of peace, and ask you to explain it. If you are unable to do so, set your lackeys to work; they may be able to do it in terms of their own "radical scientific" surface slush. The following is taken from the majority report of one of your national committees during one of your recent national conventions. It was signed by Ernest Untermann and J. Stitt Wilson, representing the West, and Joshua Wanhope, editor of the Call, and Robert Hunter, representing the East, and it was adopted as a portion of the party program. We learn from it that—

"Race feeling is not so much a result of social as of biological evolution. It does not change essentially with changes of economic systems. It is deeper than any class feeling and will outlast the capitalist system. It persists even after race prejudice has been outgrown. It exists not because the capitalists nurse it for economic reasons, but the capitalists rather have an opportunity to nurse it for economic reasons because it exists as a product of biology. It is bound to play a role in the economics of the future society. If it should not assert itself in open warfare under a Socialist form of society, it will nevertheless lead to a rivalry of races for expansion over the globe as a result of the play of natural and sexual selection. We may temper this race feeling by education, but we can never hope to extinguish it altogether. Class-consciousness must be learned, but race consciousness is inborn and cannot be wholly unlearned. A few individuals may indulge in the luxury of ignoring race and posing as utterly raceless humanitarians, but whole races never.

Where races struggle for the means of life, racial animosities cannot be avoided. Where working people struggle for jobs, self-preservation enforces its decrees. Economic and political considerations lead to racial fights and to legislation restricting the invasion of the white man's domain by other races."

It is well that the New Negro should know this, since it justifies him in giving you a taste of your own medicine. The writer of these lines is also a Socialist; but he refuses in this crisis of the world's history to put either Socialism or your party above the call of his race. And he does this on the very grounds which you yourselves have given in the document quoted above. Also because he is not a fool.

March 27th, 1920.

––––––

An Open Letter to the Socialist Party of New York City.

Gentlemen: During 1917 the white leaders of the Republican party were warned that the Negroes of this city were in a mood unfavorable to the success of their party at the polls and that this mood was likely to last

until they changed their party's attitude toward the Negro
masses. They scouted this warning because the Negroes
whom they had selected to interpret Negro sentiment for
them still confidently assured them that there had been
no change of sentiment on the part of the Negro people,
and white politicians did not think it necessary to come
and find out for themselves. Consequently they were lied
to by those whose bread and butter depended on such
lying. Then came the mayoralty campaign, and, when it
was too late they discovered their mistake. At a memor-
able meeting at Palace Casino John Purroy Mitchell, the
candidate of the Republican party, and Theodore Roosevelt, its idol, were almost hissed off the stage, while the
Mitchell outdoor speakers found it impossible to speak on
the street corners of Harlem. The party went down to
defeat and Judge Hylan was elected.

All this is recent history, and it is called to your attention at this time only because you are in danger of making
a similar costly mistake. You, too, have selected Negro
spokesmen on whose word you choose to rely for information as to the tone and temper of Negro political
sentiment. You have chosen to adopt the same faulty
method of the white Republican politicians, and you do
not care to go behind the word of your selected exponents
of Negro thought and feeling. Yet the pitiful vote which
you polled in the last election might have warned you that
something had gone wrong in your arrangements. What
that something is we shall now proceed to show you—if
you are still able to see.

During the recent world war the Negro in America was
taught that while white people spoke of patriotism, religion, democracy and other sounding themes, they remained loyal to one concept above all others, and that was
the concept of race. Even in the throes of war, and on

the battlefields of France it was "race first" with them. Out of this realization was born the new Negro ideal of "race first" for us. And today, whether Negroes be Catholics or Protestants, capitalists or wage workers, Republicans or Democrats, native or foreign-born, they begin life anew on this basis. Alike in their business alignments, their demands on the government and political parties, and in their courageous response to race rioters, they are responding to this sentiment which has been bred by the attitude of white men here and everywhere else where white rules black. To be sure, neither Burleson nor Palmer have told you or the rest of the white world this. The Angle-Saxon white man is a notorious hypocrite; and they have preferred to prate of Bolshevism—your "radicalism"—rather than tell the truth of racialism, our "radicalism," because this was an easier explanation, more in keeping with official stupidity. But we had supposed that you were intelligent enough to find this out. Evidently, you were not.

Your official Negro exponents, on behalf of their bread and butter, have seized on this widely-published official explanation to make you believe that the changed attitude of the Negro masses was due to the propaganda which you were paying them (at their published request) to preach. But this is a lie. Don't take our word for it. Do some reading on your own account. Get a hundred different Negro newspapers and magazines, outside of those which you have subsidized, and study their editorial and other pronouncements, and you will see that this is so.

But let us come nearer home. The propaganda of Socialism has been preached in times past in Harlem by different people without awakening hostility of any sort. Today it elicits a hostility which is outspoken. Send up and see; then ask yourselves the reason. You will find a

Negro Harlem reborn, with business, enterprises and cultural arrangements. And these things have been established without any help from you or those who eat your bread. Even the work of Socialist propaganda was neglected by you between 1912 and 1917. Consult your own memories and the columns of the Call.

All these things are the recent products of the principle of "race first." And among them the biggest is the Universal Negro Improvement Association, with its associate bodies, the Black Star Line and the Negro Factories Corporation. No movement among American Negroes since slavery was abolished has ever attained the gigantic proportions of this. The love and loyalty of millions go out to it as well as the cold cash of tens of thousands. Yet your Negro hirelings have seen fit to use the organs which you have given them to spread Socialist propaganda for the purpose of attacking all these things, and the Black Star Line in particular. Do you wonder now that they meet with such outspoken opposition that they have been driven to seek an underhanded alliance with the police (as your Negro Socialist organ avows in its latest issue)? Isn't that a glorious alliance for purposes of Negro propaganda? When such things can happen you may depend upon it that someone has been fooling you.

And, just as the white Republicans did, you have assumed that those whom chance or change brought your way have, somehow, achieved a monopoly of the intellect and virtue of the Negro race. Do you think that this is sound sense on your part? Of course, it was natural that they should tell you so. But was it natural for you to be so simple as to believe it? On March 27 this newspaper in an editorial quoted a passage from one of your official documents showing that the white men of your party officially put "race first" rather than "'class first," which latter phrase is your henchmen's sole contribution to "sociology"—for us. The quoted passage cuts the very heart out of their case. And yet, those whom you have selected to represent you are so green and sappy in their Socialism that, although six weeks have elapsed since this was hurled at their thick heads, not one of them has yet been able to trace to its source, this quotation from one of your own official documents. Think of it! And in the meantime you yourselves are such "easy marks" that you believe them, on their own assertion, to be the ablest among the Negroes of America. It is not easy to decide which of the two groups is the bigger joke—you or they.

You have constantly insisted that "there is no race problem, only an economic problem," but you will soon be in a fair way to find out otherwise. Some day you will, perhaps, have learned enough to cease being "suckers" for perpetual candidates who dickered with the Democrats up to within a month of "flopping" to your party only because they "couldn't make it" elsewhere; some day, perhaps, you will know enough to put Socialism's cause in the hands of those who will refrain from using your party's organ for purposes of personal pique, spite and venom. When that day dawns Socialism will have a chance to be heard by Negroes on its merits. And even now, if you should send anyone up here (black or white) to put the cause of Karl Marx, freed from admixture of rancor and hatred of the Negro's own defensive racial propaganda, you may find that it will have as good a chance of gaining adherents as any other political creed. But until you change your tactics or make your exponents change theirs your case among us will be hopeless indeed.—May, 1920.

"Patronize Your Own."

The doctrine of "Race First," although utilized largely by the Negro business men of Harlem, has never received any large general support from them. If we remember rightly, it was the direct product of the out-door and indoor lecturers who flourished in Harlem between 1914 and 1916. Not all who were radical shared this sentiment. For instance, we remember the debate between Mr. Hubert Harrison, then president of the Liberty League, and Mr. Chanler Owen, at Palace Casino in December, 1918, in which the "radical" Owen fiercely maintained "that the doctrine of race first was an indefensible doctrine"; Mr. Harrison maintaining that it was the source of salvation for the race. Both these gentlemen have run true to form ever since.

But to return to our thesis. The secondary principle of "patronize your own," flowing as it does from the main doctrine of "race first," is subject to the risk of being exploited dishonestly––particularly by business men. And business men in Harlem have shown themselves capable of doing this all the time. They seem to forget that "do unto others as you would have them do unto you" is a part of the honest application of this doctrine. Many of these men seem to want other black people to pay them for being black. They seem to think that a dirty place and imperfect service and 3 cents more a pound should be rewarded with racial patronage regardless of these demerits.

On the other hand, there have grown up in Harlem Negro businesses, groceries, ice cream parlors, etc., in which the application of prices, courtesy and selling efficiency are maintained. This is the New Negro business man, and we say "more power to him." If this method of applying the principle should continue to increase in popularity we are sure to have in Harlem and elsewhere a full and flowing tide of Negro business enterprises gladly and loyally supported by the mass of Negro purchasers to their mutual benefit.

The Negro business man who is unintelligently selfish, makes a hash of racial welfare in the attempt to achieve individual success. A case in point is that of the brown-skinned dolls. Twenty years ago the Negro child's only choice was between a white Caucasian doll and the "nigger doll." On the lower levels the one was as cheap as the other. Then, a step at a time came the picturesque poupee, variously described as the "Negro doll," the "colored doll" and the "brown-skinned doll." This was sold by white stores at an almost prohibitive price. It was made three times as easy for the Negro child to idolize a white doll as to idolize one with the features of its own race. When the principle of "Race First" began to be proclaimed from scores of platforms and pulpits, certain Negro business men saw a chance to benefit the race and, incidently to reap a wonderful harvest of profits, by appealing to a principle for whose support and maintenance, here and elsewhere, they had never paid a cent. "Factories" for the production of brown-skinned dolls began to spring up—most of the factoring consisting of receiving these dolls from white factories and either stuffing them with saw dust, excelsior or other filling, or merely changing them from one wrapper to another. Bear in mind that the proclaimed object was to make it easier for the Negro mother to teach race patriotism to her Negro child. Yet it was soon notorious that these leeches were charging $3, $4 and $5 for Negro dolls which could sell at prices ranging from 75 cents to $1.25, and yet leave a handsome margin of profit.

.The result is that today even in Negro Harlem nine out of ten Negro children are forced to play with white dolls, because rapacious scoundrels have been capitalizing the principle of "patronize your own" in a one-sided way. By lowering their prices to a reasonable level, they could extend their business tremendously. Failing to do this, they are playing into the hands of the vendors of white dolls and making it much easier for the Negro mother to select a white doll for her child; limiting at once their own market and restricting the development of a larger racial ideal.

The Women of Our Race.

America owes much to the foreigner and the Negro in America owes even more. For it was the white foreigner who first proclaimed that the only music which America had produced that was worthy of the name was Negro music. It naturally took some time for this truth to sink in, and, in the meantime, the younger element of Negroes, in their weird worship of everything that was white, neglected and despised their own race-music. More than one college class had walked out, highly insulted, when their white teachers had asked them to sing "Swing Low Sweet Chariot" and "My Lord, What a Morning." It is to be hoped that they now know better.

But the real subject of this editorial is not Negro music, but Negro women. If any foreigner should come here from Europe, Asia or Africa and be privileged to pass in review the various kinds of women who live in our America he would pick out as the superior of them all— the Negro woman. It seems a great pity that it should be left to the foreigner to "discover" the Negro-American woman. For her own mankind have been seeing her for centuries. And yet, outside of the vague rhetoric of the brethren in church and lodge when they want her to turn their functions into financial successes, and outside of Paul Dunbar and perhaps two other poets, no proper amount of esthetic appreciation of her has been forthcoming from their side.

Consider the facts of the case. The white women of America are charming to look at—in the upper social classes. But even the Negro laundress, cook or elevator-girl far surpasses her mistress in the matter of feminine charms. No white woman has a color as beautiful as the dark browns, light-browns, peach-browns, or gold and bronze of the Negro girl. These are some of the things which make a walk through any Negro section of New York or Washington such a feast of delight.

Then, there is the matter of form. The bodies and limbs of our Negro women are, on the whole, better built and better shaped than those of any other women on earth —except perhaps, the Egyptian women's. And their gait and movement would require an artist to properly describe. The grace of their carriage is inimitable.

But their most striking characteristic is a feature which even the crude mind of mere man can appreciate. It is, to quote "Gunga Din," "the way in which they carry their clothes." They dress well—not merely in the sense that their clothing is costly and good to look at; but in that higher sense in which the Parisian woman is the best-dressed woman in Europe. From shoes and stockings to shirtwaists and hats, they choose their clothes with fine taste and show them off to the best advantage when they put them on. That is why a man may walk down the avenue with a Negro cook or factory girl without anyone's being able to guess that she has to work for a living.

And, finally, in the matter of that indefinable some-

thing which, for want of a better word, we call simply
"charm"—the Negro women are far ahead of all others
in America. They have more native grace, more win-
someness, greater beauty and more fire and passion.
These facts have already begun to attract ttention, here
and elsewhere, and, eventually, the Negro woman will
come into her own.

What say you, brothers! Shall we not love her while
she is among us? Shall we not bend the knee in worship
and thank high heaven for the great good fortune which
has given us such sisters and sweethearts, mothers and
wives?

To the Young Men of My Race.

The Negro is already at work on the problems of reconstruction. He finds himself in the midst of a world
which is changing to its very foundations. Yet millions
of Negroes haven't now—and have never had—the slightest knowledge or idea of what those foundations are. How
can they render effective aid to the world without understanding something of how the world, or society, is ar-
ranged, how it runs, and how it is run?

No one, friendly or unfriendly, can deny that the
Negroes of America do wish to help in constructing this
world of men and things which will emerge from the
Great War. They want to help, because they realize that
their standing and welfare and happiness in that world
will very largely depend upon what kind of world it is.
They have not been happy, so far, in America—nor, so
far as the white man's rule is concerned,—anywhere else
under it. And they want to be happy, if that be possible.
For which reason they want to help in the re-shaping of
the world-to-be.

They feel the burdens put on them by the White Lords
of subjection and repression, of 39 cents worth of education a year in Alabama, of the deep race hatred of the
Christian Church, the Y. M. C. A. and the Associated
Press; of lynching in the land of "liberty," disfranchisement in "democratic" America, and segregation on the
Federal trains and in the Federal departments. They feel
that the world should be set free from this machinery of
mischief—for their sakes as well as that of the world.

Such is the state of mind of the Negro masses here.
And now what does this attitude of the Negro masses require? GUIDANCE! Guidance, shaping and direction.
Here is strength, here is power, here is a task to call
forth the sublimest heroism on the part of those who
should lead them. And what do we find? No guidance,
no shaping of the course for these millions. The blind
may not safely lead the blind in these critical times—and
blind men are practically all that we have as leaders.

The old men whose minds are always retrospecting and
reminiscing to the past, who were "trained" to read a few
dry and dead books which they still fondly believe are
hard to get—these do not know anything of the modern
world, its power of change and travel, and the mighty
range of its ideas. Its labor problems and their relation
to wars and alliances and diplomacy are not even suspected
by these quaint fossils. They think that they are "leading"
Negro thought, but they could serve us better if they
were cradelled in cotton-wool, wrapped in faded roses,
and laid aside in lavender as mementoes of a dead past.

The young men must gird up their loins for the task
of leadership—and leadership has its stern and necessary
duties. The first of these is TRAINING. Not in
a night did the call come to Christ, not in a day was He
made fit to make the great sacrifice. It took thirty years

of preparation to fit him for the work of three. Even so, on you, young men of Negro America, descends the duty of the great preparation. Get education. Get it not only in school and in college, but in books and newspapers, in market-places, institutions, and movements. Prepare by knowing; and never think you know until you have listened to ten others who know differently—and have survived the shock.

The young man's second duty is IRREVERENCE. Reverence is in one sense, respect for what is antiquated because it is antiquated. This race has lived in a rut too long to reverence the rut. Oldsters love ruts because they help them to "rub along," they are easy to understand; they require the minimum of exertion and brains, and they give the maximum of ease. Young man! If you wish to be spiritually alert and alive; to get the very best out of yourself—shun a rut as you would shun the plague! Never bow the knee to Baal because Baal is in power; never respect wrong and injustice because they are enshrined in "the sacred institutions of our glorious land"; never have patience with either Cowardice or Stupidity because they happen to wear venerable whiskers. Read, reason, and think on all sides of all subjects. Don't compare yourself with the runner behind you on the road; always compare yourself with the one ahead; so only will you go faster and farther. And set it before you, as a sacred duty always to surpass the teachers that taught you —and this is the essence of irreverence.

The last great duty is COURAGE. Dear man of my people, if all else should fail you, never let *that* fail. Much as you need preparation and prevision you are more in need of Courage. This has been, and is yet, A DOWN-TRODDEN RACE. Do you know what a down-trodden race needs most? If you are not sure, take down your Bible and read the whole story of Gideon and his band. You will then understand that, as Dunbar says :

"Minorities since time began
    Have shown the better side of man;
And often, in the lists of time,
    One Man has made a cause sublime."

You will learn the full force of what another American meant when he told the young men of his age:

"They are slaves who dare not choose
    Hatred, scoffing and abuse,
Rather than in silence shrink
    From the truth they needs must think,
They are slaves who dare not be
    In the right with two or three."

A people under the heels of oppression has more need of heroic souls than one for whom the world is bright. It was in Egypt and in the wilderness that Israel had need of Moses, Aaron and Joshua. No race situated like ours, has any place of leadership for those who lack courage, fortitude, heroism. You may have to turn your eyes away from the fleshpots of Egypt; you may be called on to fight with wild beasts at Ephesus; you may have to face starvation in the wilderness or crucifixion on Calvary. Have the courage to do that which the occasion demands when it comes. And I make you no promise that "in the end you will win a glorious crown." You may fail, fall and be forgotten. What of it? When you think of our heroic dead on Messines Ridge, along the Aisne and at

Chateau Thierry—how does your heart act? It thrills!
It thrills because
            "Manhood hath a larger span
            And wider privilege of life than Man."
and you, young Negro Men of America, you are striving
to give the gift of manhood to this race of ours.

The future belongs to the young men.—January, 1919.

CHAPTER VII.

OUR INTERNATIONAL CONSCIOUSNESS.

[The ideas expressed in the title of this chapter were formulated as early as 1915 when I was in the unique position of being the black leader and lecturer of a white lecture forum, organized by white liberals, radicals and others at the old Lenox Casino, at 116th St. & Lenox Ave., New York City. What white people in general thought of the value of my services at this forum can be read in a letter written by a white southerner and appearing in the New York Globe of December 15, 1920. After the closing of this lecture forum the same explanation of the racial significance of the whole process of the war was expressed in other lectures given to white people at a lecture forum which I maintained in the Brownsville section of Brooklyn. I make these explanations here because I value somewhat the point of priority in the face of Mr. Lothrop Stoddard's remarkable book, "The Rising Tide of Color Against White World-Supremacy" and the sweeping tide of racial consciousness which found expression subsequently in those Negro newspapers and magazines which have been called radical.]

The White War and the Colored World.

The newspapers which we read every day inform us that the world is at war. Searching the pages of the statisticians, we find that the world is made up of 17 hundred million people of which 12 hundred million are colored—black and brown and yellow. This vast majority is at peace and remains at peace until the white monority determines otherwise. The war in Europe is a war of the white race wherein the stakes of conflict are the titles to possession of the lands and destinies of this colored majority in Asia, Africa and the islands of the sea.

There can be no doubt that the white race as it exists today, is the superior race of the world. And it is superior, not because it has better manners more religion or a higher culture; these things are metaphysical and subject to dispute. The white race rests its claim to superiority on the frankly materialistic ground that it has the guns, soldiers, the money and resources to keep it in the position of the top-dog and to make its will go. This is what white men mean by civilization, disguise it how they may. This struggle is a conflict of wills and interests among the various nations which make up the white race, to determine whose will shall be accepted as the collective will of the white race; to decide, at least for this century, who shall be the inheritors of the lands of Africa and Asia and dictators of the lives and destinies of their colored inhabitants.

The peculiar feature of the conflict is that the white race in its fratricidal strife is burning up, eating up, consuming and destroying these very resources of ships, guns, men and money upon which its superiority is built. They are bent upon this form of self-destruction and nothing that we can say will stop them.

As representatives of one of the races constituting the colored majority of the world, we deplore the agony and blood-shed; but we find consolation in the hope that when this white world shall have been washed clean by its baptism of blood, the white race will be less able to thrust the strong hand of its sovereign will down the throats of the other races. We look for a free India and an independent Egypt; *for nationalities in Africa flying their own flags and dictating their own internal and foreign policies.* This is what we understand by "making the

world safe for democracy." Anything less than this will
fail to establish "peace on earth and good will toward
men." For the majority races cannot be eternally coerced
into accepting the sovereignity of the white race. They
are willing to live in a world which is the equal possession
of all peoples—white, black, brown and yellow. If the
white race is willing, they will live at peace with it. But
if it insists that freedom, democracy and equality are to
exist only for white men, then, there will be such blood-
shed later as this world has never seen. And there is no
certainty that in such a conflict the white race will come
out on top. Not the destinies of the world, but the destinies of the white race are in the hands of the whtie
race.—1917.

———

U-Need-a Biscuit.

There is one advertisement which appears in the magazines, on the streets and bill boards which has always
seemed to us a masterly illustration of the principle of
repetition. When going to work in the morning we look
up from our daily newspaper and see the flaring sign
which states that U-need-a Biscuit, we may ignore its
appeal the first time, but as the days go by the constant
insistence reaches our inner consciousness and we decide
that perhaps after all we do need a biscuit. At any rate,
whenever we have biscuits to buy it is natural that the
biscuit which has been most persistently advertised should
recur at once to our minds and that we should buy that
particular biscuit.

We beg to call the above apologue to the attention of
the white people of this country who guide the ship of
state either in the halls of Congress or through the
columns of the white newspapers. They are seemingly at

a loss to account for the new spirit which has come over the Negro people in the Western world. Some pretend to believe that it is Bolshevism—whatever that may be. Others tell us that it is the product of alien agitators, and yet others are coming to the front with the novel explanation that it springs from a desire to mingle our blood with that of the white people.

Perhaps we are wasting our time in offering an explanation to the white men of this country. It has been proven again and again that the Anglo-Saxon is such a professional liar that with the plain truth before his eyes he will still profess to be seeing something else. Nevertheless we make the attempt because we believe that a double benefit may accrue to us thereby. Does any reader who lived through the years from 1914 to 1919 and is still living remember what "Democracy" was? It was the U-need-a Biscuit advertised by Messrs. Woodrow Wilson, Lloyd George, Georges Clemenceau and thousands of perspiring publicists, preachers and thinkers, who were on one side of a conflict then raging in Europe.

Now, you cannot get men to go out and get killed by telling them plainly that you who are sending them want to get the other fellow's land, trade and wealth, and you are too cowardly or too intelligent to go yourself and risk getting shot over the acquisition. That would never do. So you whoop it up with any catchword which will serve as sufficient bait for the silly fools whom you keep silly in order that you may always use them in this way. "Democracy" was such a catch-word, and the honorable gentlemen to whom we referred above advertised it for all it was worth—to them. But, just as we prophesied in 1915, there was an unavoidable flare-back. When you advertise U-need-a Biscuit incessantly people will want it; and when you advertise democracy incessantly the people to whom you trumpet forth its deliciousness are likely to believe you, take you at your word, and, later on, demand that you make good and furnish them with the article for which you yourself have created the appetite.

Now, we Negroes, Egyptians and Hindus, under the pressure of democracy's commercial drummers, have developed a democratic complex which in its turbulent insistence is apt to trouble the firms for whom these drummers drummed. Because they haven't any of the goods which they advertised in the first place, and, in the second place, they haven't the slightest intention of passing any of it on—even if they had.

So, gentlemen, when you read of the Mullah, of Said Zagloul Pasha and Marcus Garvey or Casely Hayford; when you hear of Egyptian and Indian nationalist uprisings, of Black Star Lines and West Indian "seditions" —kindly remember (because *we* know) that these fruits spring from the seeds of your own sowing. You have said to us "U need a biscuit," and, after long listening to you, we have replied, "We do!" Perhaps next time—if there is a next time—you will think twice before you furnish to "inferior" peoples such a stick as "democracy" has proved for the bludgeoning of your heads. In any case your work has been too well done for even you to obliterate it. The Negro of the Western world can truthfully say to the white man and the Anglo-Saxon in particular, "You made me what I am today, I hope you're satisfied." And if the white man isn't satisfied—well, we should worry. That's all.—July, 1920.

Our Larger Duty.

The problem of the twentieth century is the problem of the Color Line. But what is the Color Line? It is the practice of the theory that the colored and "weaker" races of the earth shall not be free to follow "their own way of life and of allegiance," but shall live, work and be governed after such fashion as the dominant white race may decide. Consider for a moment the full meaning of this fact. Of the seventeen hundred million people that dwell on our earth today more than twelve hundred million are colored—black and brown and yellow. The so-called white race is, of course, the superior race. That is to say, it is on top by virtue of its control of the physical force of the world—ships, guns, soldiers, money and other resources. By virtue of this control England rules and robs India, Egypt, Africa and the West Indies; by virtue of this control we of the United States can tell Haytians, Hawaiians and Filipinos how much they shall get for their labor and what shall be done in their lands; by virtue of this control Belgium can still say to the Congolese whether they shall have their hands hacked off or their eyes gouged out—and all without any reference to what Africans, Asiatics or other inferior members of the world's majority may want.

It is thus clear that, as long as the Color Line exists, all the perfumed protestations of Democracy on the part of the white race must be simply downright lying. The cant of "Democracy" is intended as dust in the eyes of white voters, incense on the altar of their own self-love. It furnishes bait for the clever statesmen who hold the destinies of their people in their hands when they go fishing for suckers in the waters of public discussion. But it becomes more and more apparent that Hindus, Egyptians, Africans, Chinese and Haytians have taken the measure of this cant and hypocrisy. And, whatever the white world may think, it will have these peoples to deal with during this twentieth century.

In dealing with them in the past it has been considered

sufficient that the white man should listen to his own
voice alone in determining what colored peoples should
have; and he has, therefore, been trying perpetually
to "solve" the problems arising from his own assumption of the role of God. The first and still the simplest
method was to kill them off, either by slaughter pure
and simple, as in the case of the American Indians and
the Congo natives, or by forcibly changing their mode of
life, as was done by those pious prudes who killed off the
Tasmanians; or by importing among them rum, gin,
whiskey and consumption, as has been attempted in the
case of the Negroes of Africa and North America. But,
unlike the red Indians and Tasmanians, most of these
subject peoples have refused to be killed off. Their
vitality is too strong.

The second method divides itself into internal and
external treatment. The internal treatment consists in
making them work, to develop the resources of their
ancestral lands, not for themselves, but for their white
overlords, so that the national and imperial coffers may
be filled to overflowing, while the Hindu ryot, on six
cents a day, lives down to the level of the imperialist
formula:

> "The poor benighted Hindoo,
> He does the best he kin do;
>   He never aches
>   For chops and steaks
> And for clothes he makes his skin do."

The external treatment consists of girdling them with
forts and battleships and holding armies in readiness to
fly at their throats upon the least sign of "uppishness" or
"impudence."

Now, this similarity of suffering on the part of colored
folk has given, and is giving, rise to a certain similarity

of sentiment. Egypt has produced the Young Egypt movement; India, the Swadesha, the All-India Congress, and the present revolutionary movement which has lit the fuse of the powder-keg on which Britain sits in India today: Africa has her Ethiopian Movement which ranges from the Zulus and Hottentots of the Cape to the Ekoi of Nigeria; in short, the darker races, chafing under the domination of the alien whites, are everywhere showing a disposition to take Democracy at its word and to win some measure of it—for themselves.

What part in this great drama of the future are the Negroes of the Western world to play? The answer is on the knees of the gods, who often make hash of the predictions of men. But it is safe to say that, before the Negroes of the Western world can play any effective part they must first acquaint themselves with what is taking place in that larger world whose millions are in motion. They must keep well informed of the trend of that motion and of its range and possibilities. If our problem here is really a part of a great world-wide problem, we must make our attempts to solve our part link up with the attempts being made elsewhere to solve the other parts. So will we profit by a wider experience and perhaps be able to lend some assistance to that ancient Mother Land of ours to whom we may fittingly apply the words of Milton:

"Methinks I see in my mind a mighty and puissant nation, rousing herself like a strong man after sleep and shaking her invincible locks; methinks I see her like an eagle mewing her mighty youth and kindling her undazzled eyes at the full noon-day beam; methinks I see her scaling and improving her sight at the fountain itself of heavenly radiance, while the whole noise of timorous and flocking birds—with them also that love the twilight—

hover around, amazed at what she means, and in their
useless gabble would prognosticate a year of sects and
schisms."—The New Negro, August, 1919.

Help Wanted for Hayti.

While we were at war our President declared, over and
over again, that we were calling upon the flower of our
manhood to go to France and make itself into manure
in order that the world might be made safe for democracy.
Today the deluded people of the earth realize that the
accent is on the "moc(k)." Ireland, India and Egypt are
living proofs that the world has been lied to. We need
not bite our tongues about it. Those who told us that the
world would be made safe for democracy have lied to
us. All over the world men and women are finding out
that when an American President, a British Premier or a
French "tiger" speaks of "the world," he does not include
the black and brown and yellow millions, who make up
the vast majority of the earth's population. And now
the sheeted ghost of a black republic rises above the
tomb where its bones lie buried and points its silent but
accusing finger at American democracy. What can we
answer in the case of Hayti? British India and Ireland,
Turkish Armenia or Russian Poland have never presented
such ruthless savagery as has been let loose in Hayti in
a private war for which President Wilson has never had
the consent of Congress. The white daily papers speak
complacently of the repulse of "bandits." What is this
but a developing disease of the American conscience,
to put the blinkers of a catchword over the eyes of the
spirit?

The people of Hayti are being shot, sabred and bombed,
while resisting an illegal invasion of their homes, and, if

public decency is not dead in America white and black men and women will insist that Congress investigate this American Ireland.

When Ireland feels the pressure of the English heel, the Irish in America make their voices heard and help to line up American public opinion on their side. When Paderewski's government massacres Jews in Poland, the Jews of America raise money, organize committees, put the U. S. Government on the job—and get results. But when Negroes are massacred—not in Africa, but in Hayti, under American control—what do we American Negroes do? So far, nothing. But that inaction will not last. Negroes must write their Congressmen and Senators concerning the atrocity perpetrated at Port au Prince last week. They should organize committees to go before Congress and put the pitiful facts, demanding investigation, redress and punishment.

For as long as such things can be done without effective protest or redress, black people every where will refuse to believe that the democracy advertised by lying white politicians can be anything but a ghastly joke.

The Cracker in the Caribbean.

"Meanwhile the feet of civilized slayers have woven across the fair face of the earth a crimson mesh of murder and rapine. The smoke of blazing villages ascends in lurid holocaust to the bloody god of battles from the altar of human hate in the obscene temple of race prejudice."

These words, which we wrote in 1912, come back to our mind eight years later with no abatement of the awful horror which they express. And what gives a special point to them at this moment is the bloody rape of the republics of Hayti and Santo Domingo which is being perpetrated ·by the bayonets of American sailors and marinés, with the silent and shameful acquiescence of 12,000,000 American Negroes too cowardly to lift a voice in effective protest or too ignorant of political affairs to know what is taking place. What boots it that we strike heroic attitudes and talk grandiloquently of Ethiopia stretching forth her hands when we Africans of the dispersion can let the land of L'Ouverture lie like a fallen flower beneath the feet of swine?

The facts of the present situation in that hapless land are given in the current issue of *The Nation* (a white American weekly). Taken together with the accounts which we have printed from time to time, it tells a tale of shuddering horror in comparison with which the Putumayo pales into insignificance and the Congo atrocities of Belgium are tame. The two West Indian republics have been murderously assaulted; their citizens have been shot down by armed ruffians, bombed by aeroplanes, hunted into concentration camps and there starved to death. In their own land their civil liberties have been taken away, their governments have been blackjacked and their property stolen. And all this by the "cracker" statesmanship of "the South," without one word of protest from that defunct department, the Congress of the United States!

The Constitution of the United States says that the power to declare war shall belong exclusively to the Congress of the United States. But the Congress of the United States has been shamelessly ignored. In furtherance of the God-given "cracker" mandate to "keep the nigger in his place," a mere Secretary of the Navy has assumed over the head of Congress the right to conquer and annex two nations and to establish on their shores the "cracker-democracy" of his native Carolina slave-runs.

It is high time that the Negro people of the United States call the hand of Josephus Daniels by appealing to the Legislature of the United States to resume its political functions, investigate this high-handed outrage and impeach the Secretary of the Navy of high crimes and misdemeanors against the peace and good name of the United States. The ordinary excuse of cowards will not obtain in this case. We would not be violating any law—wartime or other—but, on the contrary, we should be striving to put an end to a flagrant violation of the Constitution itself on the part of a high officer, who took an oath to maintain, support and defend it. This is our right and our duty. Irishmen, on behalf of Ireland, sell the bonds of an Irish loan to free Ireland from the tyranny of Britain—with whom we are on friendly terms—on the very steps of New York's City Hall, while we black people are not manly enough to get up even a petition on behaf of our brothers in Hayti.

Out upon such crawling cowardice! Rouse, ye slaves, and show that the spirit of liberty is not quite dead among you! You who elected "delegates" to go to a Peace Conference to which you had neither passport nor invitation, on behalf of bleeding Africa, get together and present a monster petition to the American Congress, over which you have some control. Remember that George the Third engaged in a contest with these colonies because he had trouble at home. He could not defeat the Pitts, Burkes and Foxes at home, and wanted to win prestige from the colonials. Had he succeeded in setting his foot on their necks he would have returned home with increased prestige and power to bend the free spirits of

England to his will. Pitt knew this, and so did Fox and
Burke. That is why they took the side of their distant
cousins against the British king. And the British liberals
of today thank their memories for it. If the "crackers"
of the South can fasten their yoke on the necks of our
brothers overseas, then God help us Negroes in America
in the years to come!

If we were now appealing directly to the white men of
America we might dwell upon the moral aspects of the
question. But we must leave that to others. Yet we
cannot do so without recalling the words of a great poet:

> "But man, proud man,
> Drest in a little brief authority,
> Most ignorant of what he's most assured—
> His glassy essence—like an angry ape,
> Plays such fantastic tricks before high heaven
> As make the angels weep."

And we draw some slight consolation from the fact
that, even if he should escape impeachment, Josephus
Daniels must surrender up his "brief authority" in another
twelvemonth.

But we who are still free in a measure must not wait
twelve months to act. We could not do that and preserve
our racial self-respect. For—

> "Whether conscious or unconscious, yet Humanity's vast
> frame
> Through its ocean-sundered fibres feels the gush of joy
> or shame;
> In the gain or loss of one race all the rest have equal
> claim."

When Might Makes Right.

A correspondent whose letter appears elsewhere raises

the question of the relation between mental competence and property rights. "Does inability to govern destroy title to ownership?" he asks. The white race assumes an affirmative answer in every case in which the national property of darker and weaker races are concerned and deny it in cases in which their own national property interests are involved. It seems strange that whereas the disturbances occurring in our own southern states are never considered sufficient to justify the destruction of their sovereignty, on the other hand, such disturbances occurring in Hayti or Mexico are considered a sufficient reason for invasion and conquest by white Americans. The same is true of England, France and Italy. A disturbance in Alexandria, Delhi, Ashanti or the Cameroons suffices to fix upon those territories and cities the badge of inferiority and incompetence to rule themselves. The conclusion is always drawn in such cases that the white race has been called by this fortunate combination of circumstances to do the ruling for them. But similar disturbances occurring in Wales, Essen or Marseilles would never be considered as sufficient to justify the dictatorship of foreign powers in the interest of "law and order."

The truth is that "might makes right" in all these cases. White statesmen, however, often deny this at the very moment when they are using "force without stint, force to the utmost" to establish "rights" which they claim over territories, peoples, commerce and the high seas. Their characteristic hypocrisy keeps them from telling the truth as plainly as Von Bernhardi did in his now famous book, "Germany and the Next War." The "sociological" reason for this hypocrisy is the fact that they need to preach "goodness," "right" and "justice" to those over whom they rule in order that their ruling may be made easy by the consequent good behavior of the ruled. But they themselves, however good, must practice ruthlessness, injustice and the rule of the strong hand to make their governance go. It is this fact which causes intelligent Negroes, Filipinos, Chinese and Egyptians to spurn with contempt the claims which Caucasian diplomats, statesmen, writers and missionaries make on behalf of their moral superiority. They lie; they know that they lie, and now they're beginning to know that we know it also. This knowledge on our part is a loss of prestige for them, and our actions in the future, based upon this knowledge, must needs mean a loss of power for them. Which is, after all, the essential fact.

Bolshevism in Barbados.

Among the newspapers in Barbados there is a charming old lady by the name of the *Barbados Standard*. From time to time this faded creature gets worried about the signs of awakening observable in those Negroes who happen to be living in the twentieth century. Then she shakes and shivers, throws a few fits, froths at the mouth, and, spasmodically flapping her arms, yells to all and sundry that there is "Bolshevism among Negroes."

Recently this stupid old thing and its congeners have discovered evidences of a Bolshevist R—r—r—revolution in Trinidad, and, presumptively, all over the British West Indies. Now the specter which these fools fear is nothing but the shadow cast by the dark body of their own system of stiff-necked pride, stark stupidity and stubborn injustice whenever the sun of civic righteousness rises above the horizon of sloth and ignorance. But, like fools afraid of their own shadows, they point at the thing for which they alone are responsible and shriek for salvation.

We shouldn't care to suggest to them that to lie down and die would be one good way to avoid these fearful shadows, because we see the possibility of another way. Let them resolve that they will cease making a lie of every promise of liberty, democracy and self-determination that they frantically made from 1914 to 1919. Let the white Englishman learn that justice exists not only for white Englishmen, but for all men. Let him get off the black man's back, stand out of the black man's light, play the game as it should be played, and he will find very little need for wasting tons of print paper and thousands of pounds in a crusade against the specter of Bolshevism.

———

A New International.

In the eyes of our overlords internationalism is a thing of varying value. When Mr. Morgan wants to float a French or British loan in the United States; when Messrs. Wilson, Clemenceau, Lloyd George and Orlando want to stabilize their joint credit and commerce; when areas like the Belgian Congo are to be handed over to certain rulers without the consent of their inhabitants—then the pæans of praise go up to the god of "internationalism" in the temple of "civilization." But when any portion of the world's disinherited (whether white or black) seeks to join hands with other groups in the same condition, then the lords of misrule denounce the idea of internationalism as anarchy, sedition, Bolshevism and disruptive propaganda.

Why the difference? It is because the international linking up of peoples is a source of strength to those who are linked up. Naturally, the overlords want to strengthen themselves. And, quite as naturally, they wish to keep their subject masses from strengthening themselves in the same way. Today the great world-majority, made up of black, brown and yellow peoples, are stretching out their hands to each other and developing a "consciousness of kind"—as Professor Giddings would call it. They are seeking to establish their own centers of diffusion for their own internationalism, and this fact is giving night⁄mares to Downing street, the Quai d'Orsay and other centers of white capitalist internationalism.

The object of the capitalist international is to unify and standardize the exploitation of black, brown and yellow peoples in such a way that the danger to the exploiting groups of cutting each other's throats over the spoils may be reduced to a minimum. Hence the various agreements, mandates and spheres of influence. Hence the League of Nations, which is notoriously not a league of the white masses, but of their gold-braided governors. Faced by such a tendency on the part of those who bear the white man's burden for what they can get out of it, the darker peoples of the world have begun to realize that their first duty is to themselves. A similarity of suffering is producing in them a similarity of sentiment, and the temper of that sentiment is not to be mistaken.

To the white statesmen "civilization" is identical with their own overlordship, with their right and power to dictate to the darker millions what their way of life and of allegiance shall be. To this the aroused sentiment of the world's darker majority demurs. They want to be as free as England, America or France. They do not wish to be "wards of the nations" of Europe any longer. And the problem for the white statesmen of the future will be to square democracy with the subjection of this dark

majority. Can they achieve either horn of this dilemma?
Can they effect a junction of the two?

Frankly, we doubt it. Continued suppression may be
fraught with consequences disastrous to white overlordship. In any case the tendency toward an international
of the darker races cannot be set back. Increasing
enlightenment, the spread of technical science, and the
recently acquired knowledge of the weak points of white
"civilization" gained by the darker peoples during the
recent World War, are enough to negative such a sup-
position. The darker peoples will strive increasingly for
their share of sunlight, and if this is what white "civilization" opposes, then white "civilization" is likely to have
a hard time of it.

The Rising Tide of Color.

Mr. William Randolph Hearst, the ablest white pub-
licist in America, has broken loose, and, in a recent
editorial in the New York *American,* has absolutely endorsed every word of the warning recently issued by Lothrop Stoddard in his book,
"The Rising Tide of Color." In justice to Mr. Hearst,
it must be pointed out (as we ourselves did in 1916) that
he saw this handwriting on the wall long ago. Mr. Hearst
is not particularly famous as a friend of the darker races;
but one must give him credit for having seen what was
involved in the war between the white nations of Europe
and America. As far back as 1915, the present writer
was engaged in pointing out to white people that the racial
aspect of the war in Europe was easily the most important, despite the fact that no American paper, not even
Mr. Hearst's, would present that side of the matter for
the consideration of its readers. Now, however, they

are beginning to wake up—as people generally do when disaster is upon them—frantically with much screaming and flapping of arms. But, in such cases, the doom approaching is but the ripened result of deeds that have been done, and is, therefore, absolutely inescapable.

The white race has lied and strutted its way to greatness and prominence over the corpses of other peoples. It has capitalized, christianized, and made respectable, "scientific," and "natural," the fact of its dominion. It has read back into history the race relations of today, striving to make the point that previous to its advent on the stage of human history, there was no civilization or culture worthy of the name. And with minatory finger it admonishes us that if it were to pass off the stage as the controlling factor in the World's destiny, there would be no civilization or culture remaining. Naturally, we take exception to both these views, because, for the past, we know better and, for the future, we think better of the many peoples who make up the cycle of civilization.

But these conditions are not the gravest at present. The fact of most tremendous import is that the white race in trying to settle its own quarrels has called in black, brown and yellow to do its fighting for it, with the result that black, brown and yellow will learn thereby how to fight for themselves, even against those whom they were called in to assist. The white race cannot escape from its dilemma, however. If it were to decree hereafter that wars between whites should be restricted to whites alone, then we should be given the poignant spectacle of the white race continuing to cut its own throat while the increasing masses of black, brown and yellow remained unaffected by that process. "It is to laugh," as the cynical gods would say. Or, to use a trite Americanism, it is, "heads I win, tails you lose." It is thumbs down for the white race in the world's arena, and they are to be the dealers of their own death blow. Such are the consequences of conquest!

The analogies between the present situation of the white race and the situation of the Roman Empire in the fourth century of the Christian era are too many and striking to be easily ignored. Now, as then, we have "barbarians" and "super-men." Now, as then, the super-men are such in their own estimation. Now, as then, they have, as they fondly think, a monopoly of the money power, brain power and political power of the world. Now, as then, the necessities of their own selfishness and greed, constrain and compel them to share their education and their culture with the races whom they exploit. Now, as then, in the crisis of their fortunes, they must utilize the knowledge and abilities of these barbarian folk, and now, as then, this exercising of abilities on behalf of the overlord develops abilities and ambition at an equal rate; and, having given the barbarian tiger its first taste of blood, the unleashed results can not now be restrained.

In the Roman days, as in the days of Charlemagne's successors, those who hold the balances generally also wield the sword; and if *their* blood and sand determine which among the rulers shall get the prizes of victory, then these same qualities must needs urge them to take from such victors-by-proxy so much of the fruits of victory as their own needs may suggest or their own power maintain. Truly "they that take the sword shall perish by the sword."

The White War and the Colored Races.

[The following article was written in 1918 when the Great War still raged. It was written for a certain well known radical magazine; but was found to be "too radical" for publication at that time. It is given now to the Negro public partly because the underlying explanation which it offers of the root-cause of the war has not yet received treatment (even among socialistic radicals) and partly because recent events in China, India, Africa and the United States have proved the accuracy of its forecasts.]

———

The Nineteenth Christian Century saw the international expansion of capitalism—the economic system of the white peoples of Western Europe and America—and its establishment by force and fraud over the lands of the colored races, black and brown and yellow. The opening years of the Twentieth Century present us with the sorry spectacle of these same white nations cutting each other's throats to determine which of them shall enjoy the property which has been acquired. For this is the real sum and substance of the original "war aims" of the belligerents; although in conformity with Christian cunning, this is one which is never frankly avowed. Instead, we are fed with the information that they are fighting for "Kultur" and "on behalf of small nationalities." Let us look carefully at this camouflage.

THE SHAM OF "DEMOCRACY."

In the first place, we in America need not leave our own land to seek reasons for suspecting the sincerity of democratic professions. While we are waging war to establish democracy three thousand miles away, millions of Negroes are disfranchised in our own land by the "cracker" democracies of the Southern States which are more intent upon making slaves of their black fellow - citizens than upon rescuing the French and Belgians from the similar brutalities of the German Junkers. The horrible holocaust of East St. Louis was possible only in three modern States—Russia of the Romanoffs, Turkey and the United States—and it ill becomes any one of them to point a critical finger at the others.

But East St. Louis was simply the climax of a long series of butcheries perpertrated on defenseless Negroes which has made the murder rate of Christian America higher than that of heathen Africa and of every other civilized land. And, although our government can order the execution of thirteen Negro soldiers for resenting the wholesale insults to the uniform of the United States and defending their lives from civilian aggressors, not one of the murderers of black men, women and children has been executed or even ferreted out. Nor has our war Congress seen fit as yet to make lynching a Federal crime. What wonder that the Negro masses are insisting that before they can be expected to enthuse over the vague formula of making the world "safe for democracy" they must receive some assurance that their corner of the world—the South—shall first be made "safe for democracy!" Who knows but that perhaps the situation and treatment of the American Negro by our own government and people may have kept the Central Powers from believing that we meant to fight for democracy in Europe, and caused them to persist in a course which has driven us into this war in which we must spend billions of treasure and rivers of blood.

It should seem, then, that "democracy," like "Kultur," is more valuable as a battle-cry than as a real belief to be practised by those who profess it. And the plea of "small nationalities" is estopped by three facts: Ireland, Greece and Egypt, whose Khedive, Abbas Hilmi, was tumbled off his throne for failing to enthuse over the claims of "civilization" as expounded by Lord Grey.

SIR HARRY JOHNSTON SPEAKS.

But this is merely disproof. The average American citizen needs some positive proof of the assertion that this war is being waged to determine who shall dictate the destinies of the darker peoples and enjoy the usufruct of their labor and their lands. For the average American citizen is blandly ignorant of the major

facts of history and has to be told. For his benefit I present the
following statement from Sir Harry Johnston, in "The Sphere"
of London. Sir Harry Johnston is the foremost English authority
on Africa and is in a position to know something of imperial
aims.

"Rightly governed, I venture to predict that Africa will, if we
are victorious, repay us and all our allies the cost of our struggle
with Germany and Austria. The war, deny it who may, was
really fought over African questions. The Germans wished, as
the chief gain of victory, to wrest rich Morocco from French
control, to take the French Congo from France, and the Portuguese Congo from Portugal, to secure from Belgium the richest
and most extensive tract of alluvial goldfield as yet discovered.
This is an auriferous region which, properly developed, will, when
war is over, repay the hardest hit of our allies (France) all that
she has lost from the German devastation of her home lands.
The mineral wealth of trans-Zambezian Africa—freed forever,
we will hope, from the German menace—is gigantic; only
slightly exploited so far. Wealth is hidden amid the seemingly unprofitable deserts of the Sahara, Nubia, Somaliland
and Namaqua. Africa, I predict, will eventually show itself
to be the most richly endowed of all the continents in valuable vegetable and mineral substances."

There is the sum and substance of what Schopenhauer would
have called "the sufficient reason" for this war. No word of
"democracy" there, but instead the easy assumption that, as a
matter of course, the lands of black Africa belong to white
Europe and must be apportioned on the good old principle:—
"   .   .   .   the simple plan,
That he shall take who has the power,
And he must keep who can."

THE ECONOMICS OF WAR.

It is the same economic motive that has been back of every
modern war since the merchant and trading classes secured control of the powers of the modern state from the battle of Plassy
to the present world war. This is the natural and inevitable
effect of the capitalist system, of what (for want of a worse
name) we call "Christendom." For that system is based upon
the wage relationship between those who own and those who
operate the gigantic forces of land and machinery. Under this

system no capitalist employs a worker for two dollars a day unless that worker creates more than two dollars' worth of wealth for him. Only out of this surplus can profits come. If ten million workers should thus create one hundred million dollars' worth of wealth each day and get twenty or fifty millions in wages, it is obvious that they can expend only what they have received, and that, therefore, every nation whose industrial system is organized on a capitalist basis must produce a mass of surplus products over and above, not the need, but the purchasing power of the nation's producers. Before these products can return to their owners as profits they must be sold somewhere. Hence the need for foreign markets, for fields of exploitation and "spheres of influence" in "undeveloped" countries whose virgin resources are exploited in their turn after the capitalist fashion. But, since every industrial nation is seeking the same outlet for its products, clashes are inevitable and in these clashes beaks and claws—armies and navies —must come into play. Hence beaks and claws must be provided beforehand against the day of conflict, and hence the exploitation of white men in Europe and America becomes the reason for the exploitation of black and brown and yellow men in Africa and Asia. And, therefore, it is hypocritical and absurd to pretend that the capitalist nations can ever intend to abolish wars. For, as long as black men are exploited by white men in Africa, so long must white men cut each other's throats over that exploitation. And thus, the selfish and ignorant white worker's destiny is determined by the hundreds of millions of those whom he calls "niggers." "The strong too often think that they have a mortgage upon the weak; but in the domain of morals it is the other way."

THE COLOR LINE.

But economic motives have always their social side; and this exploitation of the lands and labor of colored folk expresses itself in the social theory of white domination; the theory that the worst human stocks of Montmartre, Seven Dials and the Bowery are superior to the best human stocks of Rajputana or Khartoum. And when these colored folk who make up the overwhelming majority of this world demand decent treatment for themselves, the proponents of this theory accuse them of seeking social equality. For white folk to insist upon the right to manage their own ancestral lands, free from the domination of tyrants, domestic and foreign, is variously described as "democracy" and "self-determination." For Negroes, Egyptians and Hindus to seek the same thing is impudence. What wonder, then, that the white man's rule is felt by them to rest upon a seething volcano whose slumbering fires are made up of the hundreds of millions of Chinese, Japanese, Hindus and Africans! Truly has it been said that "the problem of the 20th Century is the problem of the Color Line." And wars are not likely to end; in fact, they are likely to be wider and more terrible—so long as this theory of white domination seeks to hold down the majority of the world's people under the iron heel of racial repression.

Of course, no sane person will deny that the white race is, at present, the superior race of the world. I use the word "superior" in no cloudy, metaphysical sense, but simply to mean that they are on top and their will goes—at present. Consider this fact as the pivotal fact of the war. Then, in the light of it, consider what is happening in Europe today. The white race is superior— its will goes—because it has invented and amassed greater means for the subjugation of nature and of man than any other race. It is the top dog by virtue of its soldiers, guns, ships, money, resources and brains. Yet there in Europe it is delibertaely burning up, consuming and destroying these very soldiers, guns, ships, money, resources and brains. the very things upon which its supremacy rests. When this war is over, it will be less able to enforce its sovereign will upon the darker races of the world. Does any one believe that it will be as easy to hold down Egypt and India and Persia after the war as it was before? Hardly.

THE RACIAL RESULTS OF THE WAR.

Not only will the white race be depleted in numbers, but its quality, physical and mental, will be considerably lowered for a time. War destroys first the strongest and bravest, the best stocks, the young men who were to father the next generation. The next generation must, consequently, be fathered by the weaker stocks of the race. And thus, in physical stamina and in brain-power, they will be less equal to the task of holding down the darker millions of the world than their fathers were. This was the thought back of Mr. Hearst's objection to our entering the war. He wanted the United States to stand as the white race's reserve of man-power when Europe had been bled white.

But what will be the effect of all this upon that colored majority whose preponderant existence our newspapers ignore? In the first place, it will feel the lifting of the pressure as the iron hand of "discipline" is relaxed. And it will expand, when that pressure is removed, to the point where it will first ask, then demand, and finally secure, the right of self-determination. It will insist that, not only the white world, but the whole world, be made "safe for democracy." This will mean a self-governing Egypt, a self-governing India, and independent African states as large as Germany and France—and larger. And, as a result, there will come a shifting of the basis of international politics and business and of international control. This is the living thought that comes to me from the newspapers and books that have been written and published by colored men in Africa and Asia during the past three years. It is what I have heard from their own lips as I have talked with them. And, yet, of this thought which is inflaming the international underworld, not a word appears in the parochial press of America, which seems to think that if it can keep its own Negroes down to servile lip-service, it need not face the world-wide problem of the "Conflict of Color," as Mr. Putnam-Weale calls it.

But that the more intelligent portions of the white world are becoming distressingly conscious of it, is evident from the first great manifesto of the Russian Bolsheviki last year when they asked about Britain's subject peoples.

And the British workingmen have evidently done some thinking in their turn. In their latest declarations they seem to see the ultimate necessity of compelling their own aristocrats to forego such imperial aspirations as that of Sir Harry Johnston, and of extending the principle of self-determination even to the black people of Africa. But eyes which have for centuries been behind the blinkers of race prejudice cannot but blink and water when compelled to face the full sunlight. And Britain's workers insist that "No one will maintain that the Africans are fit for self-government." And on the same principle (of excluding the opinion of those who are most vitally concerned) Britain's ruling class may tell them that "No one maintains that the laboring classes of Britain are fit for self-government." But their half-hearted demand that an international committee shall take over the British, German, French and Portuguese possessions in Africa and manage them as independent nationalities (?)

until they can "go it alone," would suggest that their eyesight is improving.

To sum it all up, the war in Europe is the result of the desire of the white governments of Europe to exploit for their own benefit the lands and labor of the darker races, and, as the war continues, it must decrease the white man's stock of ability to do this successfully against the wishes of the inhabitants of those lands. This will result in their freedom from thralldom and the extension of political, social, and industrial democracy to the twelve hundred million black and brown and yellow peoples of the world. This, I take it, is what President Wilson had in mind when he wished to make the world "safe for democracy." But, whether I am mistaken or not, it is the idea which dominates today the thought of those darker millions.

CHAPTER VIII.

EDUCATION AND THE RACE.

[With most of the present sources of power controlled by the white race it behooves my race as well as the other subject races to learn the wisdom of the weak and to develop to the fullest that organ whereby weakness has been able to overcome strength; namely, the intellect. It is not with our teeth that we will tear the white man out of our ancestral land. It isn't with our jaws that we can ring from his hard hands consideration and respect. It must be done by the upper and not by the lower parts of our heads. Therefore, I have insisted ever since my entry into the arena of racial discussion that we Negroes must take to reading, study and the development of intelligence as we have never done before. In this respect we must pattern ourselves after the Japanese who have gone to school to Europe but have never used Europe's education to make them the apes of Europe's culture. They have absorbed, adopted, transformed and utilized, and we Negroes must do the same. The three editorials in this chapter and the article which follows them were written to indicate from time to time the duty of the transplanted African in this respect.]

Reading for Knowledge.

Some time ago we wrote an editorial entitled "Read, Read, Read!" We touch upon the same subject again, because in our recent trip to Washington we found thousands of people who are eager to get in touch with the stored-up knowledge which the books contain, but do not know just where to turn for it. In New York the same situation obtains, and no help is afforded by the papers of our race.

The reason is that some of our newspaper editors don't read and don't know beans themselves. James W. Johnson is one of the notable exceptions. We were cheered up a good deal by noting his recent editorial advice to our "leaders" to read Arthur Henderson's "The Aims of Labor." But that was six months after the editor of *The Voice* had been telling thousands of the "led" all about it and about the British Labor Party and the Russian Bolsheviki in his outdoor talks in Harlem.

But there is no doubt that the New Negro is producing a New Leadership and that this new leadership will be based not upon the ignorance of the masses, but upon their intelligence. The old leadership was possible partly because the masses were ignorant. Today the masses include educated laymen who have studied science, theology, history and economics, not, perhaps in college but, nevertheless, deeply and down to date. These young men and women are not going to follow fools and, indeed, are not going to follow *any one,* blindly. They want a reason for the things that they are asked to do and to respect. The others, the so-called Common People, are beginning to read and understand. As we sat in the great John Wesley A. M. E. Zion Church in Washington one Sunday night, and heard the cultured black minister speak to his people on literature, science, history and sociology, and yet so simply that even the dullest could catch the meat and inspiration of his great ideas, we could not help saying as we went out of the church: "Depend upon it, these people will demand as much from their next minister." In fact our race will demand as much from *all* its leaders. And they will demand no less for themselves.

So, with a glad heart, we reprint the following paragraphs from our earlier editorial trusting that our readers everywhere may find them helpful:

As a people our bent for books is not encouraging. We mostly read trash. And this is true not only of our rank and file but even of our leaders. When we heard Kelly Miller address the Sunrise Club of New York at a Broadway hotel two or three years ago, we were shocked at the ignorance of modern science and modern thought which his remarks displayed. His biology was of the brand of Pliny who lived about eighteen hundred years ago. For him Darwin and Spencer and Jacques Loeb had never existed nor written. His ignorance of the A. B. C.'s of astronomy and geology was pitiful.

If this is true of the leaders to whom our reading masses look, what can we expect from those reading masses? The masses must be taught to love good books. But to love them they must first know them. The handicaps placed on us in America are too great to allow us to ignore the help which we can get from that education which we get out of school for ourselves—the only one that is really worth while.

Without the New Knowledge the New Negro is no better than the old. And this new knowledge will be found in the books. Therefore, it would be well if every Negro of the new model were to make up his (or her) mind to get the essentials of modern science and modern thought as they are set down in the books which may be easily had. Don't talk about Darwin and Spencer: read them!

To help the good work along we append the following list of books that are essential. When you *master* these you will have a better "education" than is found in nine-tenths of the graduates of the average American college.

"Modern Science and Modern Thought," by Samuel Laing; "The Origin of Species" and "The Descent of Man," by Charles Darwin; "The Principles of Sociology" and "First Principles," by Herbert Spencer; "The Childhood of the World" and "The Childhood of Religion," by Edward Clodd; "Anthropology," by E. B. Tylor (very easy to read and a work of standard information on Races, Culture and the origins of Religion, Art and Science) ; Buckle's "History of Civilization"; Gibbon's "Decline and Fall of the Roman Empire"; "The Martyrdom of Man," by Winwood Reade; the books on Africa by Livingstone and Mungo Park, and "The Mind of Primitive Man," by Franz Boas.—Sept., 1918.

Education and the Race.

In the dark days of Russia, when the iron heel of Czarist despotism was heaviest on the necks of the people, those who wished to rule decreed that the people should remain ignorant. Loyalty to interests that were opposed to theirs was the prevailing public sentiment of the masses. In vain did the pioneers of freedom for the masses perish under the knout and the rigors of Siberia. They sacrificed to move the masses, but the masses, strong in their love of liberty, lacked the head to guide the moving feet to any successful issue. It was then that Leo Tolstoi and the other intelligentsia began to carry knowledge to the masses. Not only in the province of Tula, but in every large city, young men of university experience would assemble in secret classes of instruction, teaching them to read, to write, to know, to think and to love knowledge. Most of this work was underground at first. But it took. Thousands of educated persons gave themselves to this work—without pay: their only hope of reward lay in the future effectiveness of an instructed mass movement.

What were the results? As knowledge spread, enthusiasm was backed by brains. The Russian revolution began to be sure of itself. The workingmen of the cities studied the thing that they were "up against," gauged their own weakness and strength as well as their opponents'. The despotism of the Czar could not provoke them to a mass movement before they were ready and had the means; and when at last they moved, they swept not only the Czar's regime but the whole exploiting system upon which it stood into utter oblivion.

What does this mean to the Negro of the Western world? It may mean much, or little: that depends on him. If other men's experiences have value for the New Negro Manhood Movement it will seek now to profit by them and to bottom the new fervor of faith in itself with the solid support of knowledge. The chains snap from the limbs of the young giant as he rises, stretches himself, and sits up to take notice. But let him, for his future's sake, insist on taking notice. To drop the figure of speech, we Negroes who have shown our *manhood* must back it by our *mind*. This world, at present, is a white man's world—even in Africa. We, being what we are, want to shake loose the chains of his control from our corner of it. We must either accept his domination and our inferiority, or we must contend against it. But we go up to win; and whether we carry on that contest with ballots, bullets or business, we can not win from the white man unless we know at least as much as the white man knows. For, after all, knowledge *is* power.

But that isn't all. What kind of knowledge is it that enables white men to rule black men's lands? Is it the knowledge of Hebrew and Greek, philosophy or literature? It isn't. It is the knowledge of explosives and deadly compounds: that is chemistry. It is the knowledge which can build ships, bridges, railroads and factories: that is engineering. It is the knowledge which harnesses the visible and invisible forces of the earth and air and water: that is science, modern science. And that is what the New Negro must enlist upon his side. Let us, like the Japanese, become a race of knowledge-getters, preserving our racial soul, but digesting into it all that we can glean or grasp, so that when Israel goes up out of bondage he will be "skilled in all the learning of the Egyptians" and competent to control his destiny.

Those who have knowledge must come down from their Sinais and give it to the common people. Theirs is the great duty to simplify and make clear, to light the lamps of knowledge that the eyes of their race may see; that the feet of their people may not stumble. This is the task of the Talented Tenth.

To the masses of our people we say: Read! Get the reading habit; spend your spare time not so much in training the feet to dance, as in training the head to think. And, at the very outset, draw the line between books of opinion and books of information. Saturate your minds with the latter and you will be forming your own opinions, which will be worth ten times more to you than the opinions of the greatest minds on earth. Go to school whenever you can. If you can't go in the day, go at night. But remember always that the best college is that on your bookshelf: the best education is that on the inside of your own head. For in this work-a-day world people ask first, not "Where were you educated?" but "What do you know?" and next, "What can you do with it?" And if we of the Negro race can master modern knowledge—the kind that counts—we will be able to win for ourselves the priceless gifts of freedom and power, and we will be able to hold them against the world.

The Racial Roots of Culture.

Education is the name which we give to that process by which the ripened generation brings to bear upon the rising generation the stored-up knowledge and experience of the past and present generations to fit it for the business of life. If we are not to waste money and energy, our educational systems should shape our youth for what we intend them to become.

We Negroes, in a world in which we are the under dog, must shape our youth for living in such a world. Shall we shape them mentally to accept the status of under-dog as their predestined lot? Or shall we shape them into men and women fit for a free world? To do the former needs nothing more than continuing as we are. To do the latter is to shape their souls for continued conflict with a theory and practice in which most of the white world that surrounds them are at one.

The educational system in the United States and the West Indies was shaped by white people for white youth, and from their point of view, it fits their purpose well. Into this system came the children of Negro parents when chattel slavery was ended—and their relation to the problems of life was obviously different. The white boy and girl draw exclusively from the stored-up knowledge and experience of the past and present generations of white people to fit them for the business of being dominant whites in a world full of colored folk. The examples of valor and virtue on which their minds are fed are exclusively white examples. What wonder, then, that each generation comes to maturity with the idea imbedded in its mind that only white men are valorous and fit to rule and only white women are virtuous and entitled to chivalry, respect and protection? What wonder that they think, almost instinctively, that the Negro's proper place, nationally and internationally, is that of an inferior? It is only what we should naturally expect.

But what seems to escape attention is the fact that the Negro boy and girl, getting the same (though worse) instruction, also get from it the same notion of the Negro's place and part in life which the white children get. Is it any wonder, then, that they so readily accept the status of inferiors; that they tend to disparage themselves, and think themselves worth while only to the extent to which they look and act and think like the whites? They know nothing of the stored-up knowledge and experience of the past and present generations of Negroes in their ancestral lands, and conclude there is no such store of knowledge and experience. They readily accept the assumption that Negroes have never been anything but slaves and that they never had a glorious past as other fallen peoples like the Greeks and Persians have. And this despite the mass of collected testimony in the works of Barth, Schweinfurth, Mary Kingsley, Lady Lugard, Morel, Ludolphus, Blyden, Ellis, Ratzel, Kidd, Es-Saadi, Casely Hayford and a host of others, Negro and white.

A large part of the blame for this deplorable condition must be put upon the Negro colleges like Howard, Fisk, Livingstone and Lincoln in the United States, and Codrington, Harrison and the Mico in the West Indies. These are the institutions in which our cultural ideals and educational systems are fashioned for the shaping of the minds of the future generations of Negroes. It cannot be expected that it shall begin with the common schools; for, in spite of logic, educational ideas and ideals spread from above downwards. If we are ever to enter into the confraternity of colored peoples it should seem the duty of our Negro colleges to drop their silly smatterings of "little Latin and less Greek" and establish modern courses in Hausa and Arabic, for these are the living languages of millions of our brethern in modern Africa. Courses in Negro history and the culture of West African peoples, at least, should be given in every college that claims to be an institution of learning for Negroes. Surely an institution of learning for Negroes should not fail to be also an institution of Negro learning.

The New Negro, Sept. 1919.

The New Knowledge for the New Negro.

Quite a good deal of unnecessary dispute has been going on these days among the guardians of the inner temple as to just which form of worship is necessary at the shrine of the Goddess Knowledge. In plain English, the pundits seem to be at odds in regard to the kind of education which the Negro should have. Of course, it has long been known that the educational experts of white America were at odds with ours on the same subject; now, however, ours seem to be at odds among themselves.

The essence of the present conflict is not the easy distinction between "lower" and "higher" education, which really has no meaning in terms of educational principles, but it is rather "the knowledge of things" versus "the knowledge of words." The same conflict has been waged in England from the days of Huxley's youth to the later nineties when the London Board Schools were recognized and set the present standard of efficiency for the rest of England. The present form of the question is, "Shall education consist of Latin and Greek, literature and metaphysics, or of modern science, modern languages and modern thought?" The real essence of the question is whether we shall train our children to grapple effectively with the problem of life that lies before them, or to look longingly back upon the past standards of life and thought and consider themselves a special class because of this.

If education be, as we assert, a training for life, it must of course have its roots in the past. But so has the art of the blacksmith, the tailor, the carpenter, the bookbinder or the priest. What the classicists really seek is the domination of the form, method and aim of that training by the form, methods and aims of an earlier age.

CLASSICS, CLERICS AND CLASS CULTURE.

Perhaps an explanation of that earlier training may serve to give the real innerness of the classicists' position so that ordinary people may understand it better than the classicists themselves seem to do. In the Middle Ages, the schools of Western Europe and the subject matter of the education given in them were based upon the Latin "disciplines." Western Europe had no literature, no learning, no science of its own. It was the church—particularly the monasteries—to which men had to go to get such training as was obtainable in a barbarous age. This training was, of course, given in the tongue of the church which was Latin, the clerical language. The contact of medieval Europeans with the dark-skinned Arabs added Greek and the knowledge of Greek literature and philosophy to the earlier medieval discipline. Imbedded in this was the substance of science nurtured by the Arabs and added to by them.

The ruling classes kept their children within the treadmill of these two literatures and languages and it came to be thought that this was the indispensable training for a gentleman. But:—

"Tempora mutantur, nos et mutamur in illis."

We are in a different age, an age in which the nation, not the church, gives training to all children, and not merely to the children of aristocrats who will grow up to do nothing. The children of the people must become the doers of all that is done in the world of tomorrow, and they must be trained for this doing. Today in England, not Oxford, the home of lost ideals, but such institutions as the University of London, are the sources of that training which gives England its physicians, surgeons, inventors, business men and artists.

CLASSICISTS IGNORANT OF LATIN AND GREEK.

But the noise of the classicists may be rudely stopped by merely pointing out the hollowness of their watch words. These persons would have us believe that Latin and Greek are, in their eyes, the backbone of any education that is worth while. Very well then, let us take them at their word. I make the broad assertion that not one in one thousand of them can read a page of Greek or Latin that may be set before them. I offer to put under their noses a page of Athenaeus or Horace (to say nothing of more important classical authors) and if they should be able to read and translate it at sight I shall be genuinely surprised. Let the common reader who is a man of today make the test with this little bit of Latin verse:

"*Exegi momentum acre perennius*
Regalique situ pyramidum altius."

Let him ask some classicist to translate off-hand this common school boy's tag from a most popular author and note whether they can place the author or translate the lines. Here is another:

Per varios casus, per tot discrimina rerum,
Tendimus in Latium.

To speak in plain United States, when it comes to the show-down it will be found that those of us who argue in favor of the modern discipline (in so far as we have any knowledge of classical literature) know more about them than those whose sole defence they are.

It is said by the classicists that a knowledge of Latin and Greek is necessary to an adequate comprehension of the English language. But so is the knowledge of Sanscrit, Arabic, French and Italian. And when it comes to facility and clearness of expression, it will be found that Huxley's prose is superior to that of Matthew Arnold, and Brisbane's superior to that of any professor of the Latin language in Harvard or Yale. So much for the ghost fighters. *Requiescant in pace!*

THE KNOWLEDGE WE NEED.

Now, what is the knowledge which the New Negro needs most? He needs above all else a knowledge of the wider world and of the long past. But that is history, modern and ancient: History as written by Herodotus and John Bach McMaster; sociology not as conceived by Giddings, but as presented by Spencer and Ward, and anthroplology as worked out by Boas and Thomas. The Negro needs also the knowledge of the best thought; but that is literature as conceived, not as a collection of flowers from the tree of life, but as its garnered fruit. And, finally, the Negro needs a knowledge of his own kind, concerning which we shall have something to say later. And the purposes of this knowledge? They are, to know our place in the human processus, to strengthen our minds by contact with the best and most useful thought-products evolved during the long rise of man from anthropoid to scientist; to inspire our souls and to lift our race industrially, commercially, intellectually to the level of the best that there is in the world about us. For *never until the Negro's knowledge of nitrates and engineering, of chemistry and agriculture, of history, science and business is on a level, at least, with that of the whites, will the Negro be able to measure arms successfully with them.*

CHAPTER NINE.

A FEW BOOKS.

The Negro in History and Civilization

(From Superman to Man, by J. A. Rogers.)

This volume by Mr. Rogers is the greatest little book on the Negro that we remember to have read. It makes no great parade of being "scientific," as so many of our young writers do who seem to think that science consists solely in logical analysis. If science consists fundamentally of facts, of information and of principles derived from those facts, then the volume before us is one of the most scientific that has been produced by a Negro writer. It sweeps the circle of all the social sciences. History, sociology, anthropology, psychology, economics and politics—even theology—are laid under contribution and yield a store of information which is worked up into a presentation so plain and clear that the simplest can read and understand it, and yet so fortified by proofs from the greatest standard authorities of the past and present that there is no joint in its armor in which the keenest spear of a white scientist may enter.

Unlike an older type of scholar (now almost extinct) the author does not go to vapid verbal philosophers or devotional dreamers for the facts of history and ethnology. He goes to historians and ethnologists for them and to anthropologists for his anthropology. The result is information which stands the searching tests of any inquirer who chooses to doubt and investigate before accepting what is set before him.

From this book the unlearned reader of the African race can gather proof that his race has not always been a subject or inferior race. He has the authority of Professor Reisner, of Harvard; of Felix Dubois, Volney, Herodotus, Finot, Sergi, the modern Egyptologists and the scholars of the white world who assembled at the Universal Races Congress in London in 1911,

for the belief that his race has founded great civilizations, has
ruled over areas as large as all Europe, and was prolific in statesmen, scientists, poets, conquerors, religious and political leaders,
arts and crafts, industry and commerce when the white race was
wallowing in barbarism or sunk in savagery. Here he can learn
on good authority, from St. Jerome and Cicero, Herodotus and
Homer down to the modern students of race history, that canni-
balism has been a practise among white populations like the
Scythians, Scots and Britons; that the white races have been
slaves; that here in America the slavery of white men was a
fact as late as the 19th century, and "according to Professor
Cigrand, Grover Cleveland's grandfather, Richard Falley, was an
Irish slave in Connecticut." In short, he will learn here, not that
newspaper science which keeps even "educated" Americans so
complacently ignorant, but the science of the scientists themselves. He will learn all that this kind of science has to tell of
the relative capacity and standing of the black and white races—
and much of it will surprise him. But all of it will please and in-
struct.

The book also deals with the facts of the present position of
the Negro in America and the West Indies; with questions of
religion, education, politics and political parties, war work,
lynching, miscegenation on both sides, the beauty of Negro
women and race prejudice. And on everyone of these topics
it gives a minimum of opinion and a maximum of information.
This information flows forth during the course of a series of dis-
cussions between an educated Negro Pullman porter and a
Southern white statesman on a train running between Chicago
and San Francisco. The superior urbanity of the Negro, coupled
with his wider information and higher intelligence, eventually
wins over the Caucasian to admit that the whole mental attitude
of himself and his race in regard to the Negro was wrong and
based on nothing better than prejudice.

This conversational device gives the author an opportunity to
present all the conflicting views on both sides of the Color Line,
and the result is a wealth of information which makes this book
a necessity on the bookshelf of everyone, Negro or Caucasian,
who has some use for knowledge on the subject of the Negro.
The book is published by the author at 4700 State Street,
Chicago.

"Darkwater."

By W. E. B. Du Bois.

An unwritten law has existed for a long time to the effect that the critical estimates which fix the status of a book by a Negro author shall be written by white men. Praise or blame—the elementary criticism which expresses only the reviewer's feelings in reference to the book—has generally been the sole function of the Negro critic. And the results have not been good. For, in the first place, white critics (except in music) have been too prone to judge the product of a Negro author as Dr. Johnson judged the dancing dog: "It isn't at all like dancing; but then, one shouldn't expect more from a dog." That is why many Negro poets of fifth grade merit are able to marshal ecomiums by the bushel from friendly white critics who ought to know better. On the other hand, there is the danger of disparagement arising solely from racial prejudice and the Caucasian refusal to take Negro literary products seriously.

In either case the work fails to secure consideration solely on its merits. Wherefore, it is high time that competent appraisal of Negro books should come from "our side of the street." But, then, the Negro reading public should be taught what to expect, viz., that criticism is neither "knocking" nor "boosting"; but an attempt, in the first place, to furnish a correct and adequate idea of the scope and literary method of the book under review, of the author's success in realizing his objects, and of the spirit in which he does his work. In the second place, the critic should be expected to bring his own understanding of the subject matter of the book to bear upon the problem of enlightening the readers' understanding, that at the end the reader may decide whether the work is worth his particular while.

This book of Dr. Du Bois' is one which challenges the swing of seasoned judgment and appraisal. It challenges also free thinking and plain speaking. For, at the very outset, we find ourselves forced to demur to the publishers' assumptions as to its author's status. "Even more than the late Booker Washington, Mr. Du Bois is now chief spokesman of the two hundred million men and women of

African blood." So say the publishers—or the author. But this is outrageously untrue. Once upon a time Dr. Du Bois held a sort of spiritual primacy among The Talented Tenth, not at all comparable to that of Booker Washington in scope, but vital and compelling for all that. The power of that leadership, however, instead of increasing since Mr. Washington's death, has decreased, and is now openly flouted by the most active and outspoken members of The Talented Tenth in Negro America. And, outside of the twelve or fifteen millions "of African blood" in the United States, the mass of that race in South and West Africa, Egypt and the Philippines know, unfortunately, very little of Dr. Du Bois. It may be, however, that this is merely a publishers' rhodomontade.

And it is the publishers themselves who challenge for this volume a comparison with "The Souls of Black Folk," which was published by McClurg in 1903. It is regrettable that they should force the issue, for "The Souls of Black Folk" is a greater book than "Darkwater" in many ways. In the first place, its high standard of craftsmanship is maintained through every chapter and page. There are no fag-ends, as in the chapter "Of Beauty and Death" in the present volume, where the rhetoric bogs down, the author loses the thread of his purpose and goes spieling off into space, spinning a series of incongruous purple patches whose tawdry glitter shows the same reversion to crude barbarism in taste which leads a Florida fieldhand to don opal-colored trousers, a pink tie, pari-colored shirt and yellow shoes. Artistically, that chapter is an awful thing, and I trust that the author is artist enough to be ashamed of it.

And, though it may savor of anti-climax, "The Souls of Black Folk" was more artistically "gotten" up—to use the grammar of its author. "Darkwater" is cheaply bound and cheaply printed on paper which is almost down to the level of the Sea-side Library. Neither in mechanical nor mental quality does the book of 1920 come up to the level of that of 1903.

Yet, in spite of some defects, "Darkwater" (with the exception of chapters six, seven, eight and nine) is a book well worth reading. It is a collection of papers written at different times, between 1908 and 1920, and strung loosely on the string of race. One wishes that the author could have included his earlier essay on The Talented Tenth and his address on the aims and ideals of modern education, delivered some twelve years ago to the colored school children of Washington, D. C.

Each paper makes a separate chapter, and each chapter is followed by a rhetorical sprig of symbolism in prose or verse in which the tone-color of the preceeding piece is made manifest to the reader. Of these tone-poems in prose and verse, the best are the Credo; A Litany at Atlanta; The Riddle of the Sphinx, and Jesus Christ in Texas. In these the lyrical quality of the author's prose is lifted to high levels. In these elegance does not slop over into turgid declamation and rhetorical claptrap—which has become a common fault of the author's recent prose as shown in The Crisis. In this, the first part of the book, the work is genuine and its rhetoric rings true. Nevertheless, the sustained artistic swing of "The Souls of Black Folk," which placed that work (as a matter of form and style) on the level of Edgar Saltus' *Imperial Purple*—this is not attained in "Darkwater."

The book may be said to deal largely with the broad international aspects of the problem of the color line and its reactions on statecraft, welt-politik, international peace and international trade, industry, education and the brotherhood of man. Each chapter, or paper, is devoted to one of these reactions. Then there is a charming autobiographical paper, "The Shadow of Years," which first appeared in The Crisis about three years ago, in which we have the study of a soul by itself. The growth of the author's mind under the bewildering shadow cast by the color line is tragically set forth. I say tragically with deliberation; for what we see here, despite its fine disguise, is the smoldering resentment of a mulatto who finds the beckoning white doors of the world barred on his approach. One senses the thought that, if they had remained open, the gifted spirit would have entered and made his home within them. *Mais, chacun a son gout,* and no one has the right to quarrel with the author on that doubtful score.

In the chapter on "The Souls of White Folk" we have a fine piece, not so much of analysis, as of exposition. The author puts his best into it. And yet that best seems to have failed to bite with acid brutality into the essential iron of the white man's soul. For the basic elements of that soul are Hypocrisy, Greed and Cruelty. True, the author brings this out; but he doesn't burn it in. The indictment is presented in terms of an appeal to shocked sensibilities and a moral sense which exists, for the white man, only in print; whereas it might have been made in other terms which come nearer to his self-love. Nevertheless it is unanswerable in its logic.

In "The Hands of Ethiopia," as in "The Souls of White Folk," we catch the stern note of that threat which (disguise it as our journals will), the colored races are making, of an ultimate appeal in terms of color and race to the white man's only God—the God of Armed Force. But the author never reaches the height of that newer thought—an international alliance of Black, Brown and Yellow against the arrogance of White.

In "Work and Wealth" and "The Servant in the House" the problems of work and its reward, and the tragedy of that reward, are grippingly set forth in relation to the Negro in America and in the civilized world. · "The Ruling of Men" is followed by three papers of very inferior merit and the book ends with a fantastic short story, "The Comet" which, like "The Coming of John" in "The Souls of Black Folk," suggests that Dr. Du Bois could be a compelling writer of this shorter form of fiction. The touch in this story of incident is light, but arresting.

Dr. Du Bois, in the looseness of phrase current in our time in America, is called a scholar—on what grounds we are not informed. But Dr. Du Bois is not a scholar; his claim to consideration rests upon a different basis, but one no less high. And when the Negro culture of the next century shall assay the products of our own it will seem remarkable that this supreme wizard of words, this splendid literary artist, should have left his own demesne to claim the crown of scholarship. Surely, there is honest credit enough in being what he is, our foremost man of culture. And this "Darkwater," despite its lapses from artistic grace, helps to rivet his claim to that consideration. It is a book which will well repay reading.

―――――

The Rising Tide of Color Against White World Supremacy.
By Lothrop Stoddard.

About ten years ago Mr. B. L. Putnam Weale in "The Conflict of Color" tried to open the eyes of the white men of the world to the fact that they were acting as their own grave diggers.

About the same time Mr. Melville E. Stone, president of the Associated Press, in an address before the Quill Club on "Race Prejudice in the Far East" reinforced the same grisly truth. Five years later "T. Shirby Hodge" wrote "The White Man's Burden: A Satirical Forecast," and ended it with these pregnant words: "The white man's burden is—himself." His publishers practically suppressed his book, which, by the way, should have been in the library of every intelligent Negro. The white world was indisposed then to listen to its voices of warning. But today the physical, economic and racial ravages of the World War have so changed the white world's mind that within four weeks of its appearance "The Rising Tide of Color Against White World Supremacy," by Lothrop Stoddard, has struck the bull's-eye of attention and has already become the most widely talked-of book of the year. White men of power are discussing its facts and its conclusions with bated breath and considerable disquietude.

Here is a book written by a white man which causes white men to shiver. For it calls their attention to the writing on the wall. It proves that the white race in its mad struggle for dominion over others has been exhausting its vital resoures and is exhausting them further. It proves to the hilt the thesis advanced in 1917 in my brief essay on "The White War and the Colored Races" that, whereas the white race was on top by virtue of its guns, ships, money, intellect and massed man-power, in the World War it was busy burning up, depleting and destroying these very resources on which its primacy depended. But even though the white capitalists knew all this their mad greed was still their master. This great race is still so low spiritually that it sells even its racial integrity for dollars and cents. Mr. Stoddard's book may disturb its sense of security for a brief space, but it cannot keep white "civilization" from its mad dance of death. "What shall it profit a man if he gain the whole world and lose his own soul?" And the white race will finally find that this is even more true racially than individually.

We have noticed for many years that whereas domestic journalism was merely journalism—the passing register of parochial sensations—the journalism of the international publicists like Lord Bryce, Meredith Townsend, Archibald Colquhoon, Putnam Weale and Hyndman was something more solid than journalism. In the writings of these men hard fact and stark reality are

wedded to wide reading and deep thinking. They are the real
social scientists rather than the stay-at-home, cloistered sociolo-
gists who, presuming to know everything, have seen nothing.
The present volume is one of the best of the former and is full of
the qualities of its class. But at the very outset it suffers from
the unwelcome assistance of Dr. Madison Grant, "chairman of the
New York Zoological Society and trustee of the American
Museum of Natural History." Dr. Grant has accumulated a
large stock of musty ethnological ideas of which he unburdens
himself in what he evidently intends as a "learned" introduction,
without which freightage the book would be much better. The
difference in value and accuracy between Mr. Stoddard's text and
the pseudo-scientific introduction of Dr. Grant would furnish
fair material for philosophic satire. Unfortunately we cannot
indulge the inclination in the columns of a weekly newspaper.

Dr. Grant, in owlish innocence, splutters out the usual futile
folly which (in other domains) has brought the white race to
the frontiers of the present crisis. He reads back into history
the racial values of today and trails the Anglo-Saxon's crass con-
ceit and arrogance across the pages of its record, finding "con-
trast of mental and spiritual endowments . . . elusive of
definition," and other racial clap-trap whose falsity has been
demonstrated again and again by warm-hearted enthusiasts like
Jean Finot and coldly critical and scientific scholars like Dr.
Taylor ("Origin of the Aryans"), Sergi ("The Mediterranean
Race") and J. M. Robertson ("The Evolution of States"). But
one can forgive Dr. Grant; he is a good American, and good
Americans (especially "scientists" on race) are usually fifty
years behind the English, who, in turn, are usually twenty years
behind the Germans. Dr. Grant's annexation of the past history
of human culture to the swollen record of the whites sounds
good—even if it smells bad. And he is in good Anglo-Saxon
company. Sir Harry Johnston does the same thing and gets titles
(scientific and other) by so doing. The Englishman takes the
very Egyptians, Hindus and tribal Liberians, whom he would
call "niggers" in New York and London, and as soon as he finds
that they have done anything worth while he tags them with a
"white" tag. Thus, to the professional "scientist" like Dr. Grant,
living in the parochial atmosphere of the United States, science
is something arcane, recondite and off the earth; while to the

American like Mr. Stoddard, who has been broadened by travel and contact with the wider world, science, is, as it should be, organized daily knowledge and common sense. Thus journalists, good and bad, are the ones who form opinion in America, because "scientists" are so distressingly stupid.

Mr. Stoddard's thesis starts from the proposition that of the seventeen hundred million people on our earth today the great majority is made up of black, brown, red and yellow people. The white race, being in the minority, still dominates over the lands of black, brown, red and (in the case of China) has assumed a right of dictatorship and disposal even in the yellow man's lands. In the course of this dictatorship and domination the white race has erected the barrier of the color line to keep the other races in their place. But this barrier is cracking and giving way at many points and the flood of racial self-assertion, hitherto dammed up, threatens to overflow the outer and inner dikes and sweep away the domination of the whites.

The author approaches his theme with a curiously graduated respect for other races. This respect, while it is a novelty in the attitude of the blond overlords, is always in direct proportion to the present power and discernible potentialities of the races discussed. For the yellow man of Japan and China he shows the greatest deference. The browns (of India, Persia, Afghanistan, Egypt and the Mohammedan world in general) are, of course, inferior, but must be respected for their militancy. The reds (the original American stock which is the backbone of the population of Mexico, Central and South America) are a source of contamination for white blood and an infernal nuisance, capable of uniting with Japan and China in an onslaught on the land areas reserved for white exploitation in the western world; while the blacks, at the foot of the ladder, have never amounted to anything, don't amount to anything now, and can never seriously menace the superiority of the whites.

The gradation is full of meaning, especially to those fervid theorists who affect to believe that religion, morality, loyalty and good citizenship constitute a good claim to the white man's respect. For it is Japan's actual military might and China's impending military might which have put them in Grade A, while the brown man's show of resistance in Egypt, India and elsewhere under Islam, and his general physical unrest and

active discontent have secured for him a classification in Grade
B.   The American in Mexico and South America keeps his window open toward the east; but the black man still seems, in our
author's eyes, to be the same loyal, gentle, stupid beast of burden
that the white man's history has known—except in those parts
of Africa in which he has accepted the Mohammedan religion and
thus become a part of the potential terror of the Moslem world.
In this we think our author mistaken; but, after all, it is neither
arguments nor logic that will determine these matters, but deeds
and accomplishments.

But, however his racial respect may be apportioned, Mr. Stoddard holds that his race is doomed.   "If the present drift be not
changed we whites are all ultimately doomed.   Unless we set our
house in order the doom will sooner or later overtake us all."
The present reviewer stakes his money on "the doom," for the
white race's disease is an ingrowing one whose development
inheres in their very nature.   They are so singularly constituted
that they would rather tear themselves to pieces parading as the
lords of creation than see any other people achieve an equal
favor of fortune.

In the pages of this book the author presents many chastening
truths and wide vistas of international politics which are enlightening when carefully studied.   But it is not our intent to cover the
entire field of his work, and we think that we have said enough
to indicate the high value and suggestiveness of the work.   But
we may be allowed to point out that all the way through the
author, though clear and enlightened, remains an unreconstructed
Anglo-Saxon, desirous of opening the eyes of his race to the
dangers which beset them through their racial injustice and
arrogance; but sternly, resolutely, intent that they shall not
share their overlordship with any other of the sons of earth.
His book is written in a clear and commendable style; he shows
but few defects of temper and a shrewd mastery of his mate-
rials.   The book should be widely read by intelligent men of
color from Tokio to Tallahassee.   It is published by Charles
Scribner's Sons at $3, and is well worth the price.

The Black Man's Burden

(*A Reply to Rudyard Kipling.*)

By HUBERT H. HARRISON.

Take up the Black Man's burden—
   Send forth the worst ye breed,
And bind our sons in shackles
   To serve your selfish greed;
To wait in heavy harness
   Be-devilled and beguiled
Until the Fates remove you
   From a world you have defiled.

Take up the Black Man's burden—
   Your lies may still abide
To veil the threat of terror
   And check our racial pride;
Your cannon, church and courthouse
   May still our sons constrain
To seek the white man's profit
   And work the white man's gain.

Take up the Black Man's burden—
   Reach out and hog the earth,
And leave your workers hungry
   In the country of their birth;
Then, when your goal is nearest,
   The end for which you fought,
Watch other's trained efficiency
   Bring all your hope to naught.

Take up the Black Man's burden—
   Reduce their chiefs and kings
To toil of serf and sweeper
   The lot of common things:
Sodden their soil with slaughter,
   Ravish their lands with lead;
Go, sign them with your living
   And seal them with your dead.

Take up the Black Man's burden—
    And reap your old reward:
The curse of those ye cozen,
    The hate of those ye barred
From your Canadian cities
    And your Australian ports;
And when they ask for meat and drink
    Go, girdle them with forts.

Take up the Black Man's burden—
    Ye cannot stoop to less.
Will not your fraud of "freedom"
    Still cloak your greediness?
But, by the gods ye worship,
    And by the deeds ye do,
These silent, sullen peoples
    Shall weigh your gods and you.

Take up the Black Man's burden—
    Until the tale is told,
Until the balances of hate
    Bear down the beam of gold.
And while ye wait remember
    That justice, though delayed,
Will hold you as her debtor
    Till the Black Man's debt is paid.